Mastering Web Development

A Journey through HTML, CSS, and JavaScript

Author: Martin Hander

Publishing Date 20231010

Pictures: pixabay.com

Preface

Welcome to "Web Development with HTML, CSS, and JavaScript." In today's digital age, the web plays a pivotal role in our lives, from serving as a source of information and entertainment to facilitating communication, commerce, and collaboration. As the backbone of this digital universe, web development has emerged as a dynamic and essential skill.

This book is your gateway to the fascinating and ever-evolving world of web development. Whether you're an aspiring web developer looking to start your journey or an experienced coder seeking to broaden your skill set, this comprehensive guide is designed to empower you with the knowledge and tools needed to create stunning, functional, and user-friendly websites and web applications.

Why This Book?

The web development landscape can be daunting, with a myriad of technologies, frameworks, and best practices to navigate. We've crafted this book to demystify the process and provide you with a clear roadmap to success. Our goal is to make web development accessible and enjoyable, whether you're building a personal project, launching a business website, or pursuing a career in the field.

What You'll Learn

In the pages that follow, you'll embark on a journey through the core technologies of web development:

- **HTML (HyperText Markup Language):** Learn how to structure the content of your web pages using HTML, the foundation of the web.

- **CSS (Cascading Style Sheets):** Discover the art of styling and design with CSS, breathing life and personality into your web projects.

- **JavaScript:** Dive into the world of programming with JavaScript, a versatile language that enables interactive and dynamic web experiences.

How This Book Is Organized

This book is divided into several chapters, each focusing on a specific aspect of web development. We'll start with the basics, gradually building your understanding of HTML, CSS, and JavaScript. As you progress, you'll explore advanced topics, best practices, and emerging trends in the field.

Each chapter is designed to be informative and practical, with hands-on examples and exercises to reinforce your learning. Whether you're a visual learner who thrives on code snippets and diagrams or someone who prefers in-depth explanations, this book caters to various learning styles.

Who This Book Is For

This book is for anyone with an interest in web development, regardless of your background or experience. Whether you're a complete beginner or an experienced programmer looking to expand your skill set, you'll find valuable insights and guidance here. The only prerequisites are curiosity, a willingness to learn, and a passion for crafting amazing web experiences.

What's Inside

- Clear explanations of fundamental concepts in web development.
- Practical examples and code snippets to reinforce your learning.
- Tips, best practices, and real-world insights from experienced developers.
- Guidance on web development tools, libraries, and frameworks.

Join the Web Development Community

Web development is not just about writing code; it's about joining a vibrant and supportive community of developers, designers, and enthusiasts. Throughout this journey, you'll find opportunities to collaborate, share knowledge, and seek help from fellow developers. The web development community is known for its openness and willingness to help others succeed.

Let's Begin!

Are you ready to embark on your web development journey? Whether you're aiming to build personal projects, launch your dream website, or pursue a career in the ever-evolving tech industry, this book is your trusty companion. Together, we'll explore the intricacies of HTML, CSS, and JavaScript, unlocking the power to create remarkable web experiences.

So, flip the page and let's dive into the exciting world of web development! The web is waiting for your creativity and innovation, and we're here to guide you every step of the way.

About the Author

The author of "Web Development with HTML, CSS, and JavaScript" brings over two decades of experience in the world of software development to this comprehensive guide. With a strong foundation in computer science and a passion for coding, the author has embarked on a journey that spans various computer languages, industries, and roles.

A Journey of Expertise

Having earned a diploma in computer science, the author's educational background laid the groundwork for a successful career in software development. From the very beginning, a curiosity for technology and an innate talent for problem-solving set the author on a trajectory of continuous learning and growth.

Over the years, the author has had the privilege of working with diverse technologies and programming languages, adapting to the ever-changing landscape of the tech industry. This breadth of experience has honed the author's ability to tackle complex challenges and deliver innovative solutions.

A Career of Innovation

The author's career has been marked by a series of achievements, each contributing to a deep reservoir of knowledge and expertise. Whether developing mission-critical software for enterprises, crafting user-friendly applications, or exploring emerging technologies, the author's dedication to excellence has consistently shone through.

The journey of software development has led the author to collaborate with a multitude of companies, each with its unique set of demands and opportunities. This exposure to diverse industries and domains has enriched the author's understanding of how technology can be harnessed to drive progress and innovation.

A Passion for Teaching

Beyond the realm of coding and software development, the author possesses a genuine passion for teaching and sharing knowledge. This book is a testament to the author's commitment to helping others embark on their own journeys in web development. With a knack for breaking down complex concepts into digestible, actionable insights, the author seeks to empower readers to unlock their full potential in the world of web development.

Join the Author on this Journey

As you delve into the pages of "Web Development with HTML, CSS, and JavaScript," you'll have the opportunity to tap into the author's wealth of experience and insights. Together with the author, you'll explore the intricacies of web development and gain the skills needed to craft exceptional web experiences.

The author's dedication to the craft of software development, coupled with a genuine desire to nurture the next generation of web developers, makes this book not just an educational resource but a companion on your own journey of discovery and achievement in the exciting and dynamic field of web development.

Table of Contents

Introduction

In the ever-evolving realm of technology, the web remains a dynamic and limitless canvas for innovation. As the digital world continues to expand, so too does the demand for skilled artisans who can craft the online experiences we encounter every day. Welcome to "Mastering Web Development: A Journey through HTML, CSS, and JavaScript" a comprehensive guide that invites you to embark on an exciting voyage into the world of web development.

In an era where the web is not just a platform but a way of life, understanding the building blocks of the internet is both empowering and essential. This book is your compass on this journey, providing the knowledge and skills you need to create captivating and functional websites from scratch. Whether you're a complete novice taking your first steps into web development or a seasoned developer looking to enhance your skills, this book offers a wealth of insights, practical guidance, and hands-on exercises to empower you on your path to mastery.

The Triumvirate of Web Development

At the heart of modern web development lies a powerful trio: HTML, CSS, and JavaScript. These three technologies form the cornerstone of every web page, combining structure, style, and interactivity to bring digital experiences to life.

- **HTML (Hypertext Markup Language)** is the bedrock of web content. With it, you define the structure of a webpage, creating headings, paragraphs, lists, forms, and more. HTML is the essential language that gives meaning to your content.

- **CSS (Cascading Style Sheets)** is the artist's palette. It lets you paint the visual style of your webpage, from fonts and colors to layouts and responsive design. CSS breathes life into the structure, making your pages not just functional but visually stunning.

- **JavaScript**, the language of interactivity, empowers you to add behavior and functionality to your websites. With JavaScript, you can create everything from simple animations to complex web applications, making the web dynamic and responsive.

Together, these technologies form the foundation of the web, and in this book, you will learn how to wield them with confidence and creativity.

Why This Book?

"Mastering Web Development" is more than just a technical manual; it's a comprehensive guide that takes you on a journey of discovery. Here's what you can expect:

- **Progressive Learning:** We'll start with the fundamentals and progressively delve into more advanced topics. Whether you're a beginner or an experienced developer, there's something here for you.

- **Hands-on Practice:** Learning by doing is at the core of this book. You'll find practical exercises and real-world examples that reinforce your understanding and help you build a strong foundation.

- **Best Practices:** Web development is more than just writing code; it's about writing good code. You'll learn industry best practices for creating maintainable, efficient, and accessible websites.

- **Web Design:** We don't just focus on code; we also explore design principles, responsive design, and user experience to help you create visually pleasing and user-friendly websites.

- **Real-world Projects:** You'll work on projects that simulate real-world scenarios, from creating a personal portfolio website to building a dynamic web application.

- **The Web Ecosystem:** Beyond HTML, CSS, and JavaScript, you'll also explore tools, libraries, and best practices that are prevalent in the modern web development landscape.

- **Future-proofing:** The web is always evolving. We'll discuss emerging trends and technologies to help you stay current in this ever-changing field.

Web development is not just a skill; it's a gateway to creativity, innovation, and limitless possibilities. By the time you finish this book, you'll be equipped with the knowledge and skills to craft your own digital masterpieces and navigate the dynamic world of web development with confidence. So, without further ado, let's embark on this exciting journey to mastering web development.

Setting Up Your Development Environment

Before we embark on our journey into the captivating world of web development with HTML, CSS, and JavaScript, there's one essential step we must take—setting up our development environment. Much like a painter prepares their canvas and gathers their brushes, a web developer must create a workspace conducive to creativity and productivity. In this chapter, we will guide you through the process of establishing a development environment tailored to your needs.

The Digital Workshop

Imagine your development environment as a digital workshop, a space where your ideas will take shape, evolve, and come to life on the canvas of the web. Your workspace should be efficient, comfortable, and equipped with the necessary tools. Let's begin by understanding what you'll need:

1. **Text Editor or Integrated Development Environment (IDE)**: Your choice of a text editor or IDE is your most critical decision. Text editors like Visual Studio Code, Sublime Text, or Atom are lightweight and highly customizable, while IDEs like WebStorm or Visual Studio offer extensive features for web development. Select the one that suits your workflow and preferences.

2. **Web Browser**: A web developer's browser is more than a tool for browsing; it's an indispensable debugging and testing platform. Chrome, Firefox, and Edge offer robust developer tools for inspecting, debugging, and testing your web projects.

3. **Version Control System (VCS)**: Collaborative and efficient development often requires version control. Git, a distributed VCS, is widely used in the industry. Platforms like GitHub, GitLab, and Bitbucket provide hosting and collaboration features for your projects.

4. **Terminal/Command Line Interface (CLI)**: Familiarize yourself with the terminal or command prompt on your operating system. This tool will be your gateway to executing commands, managing files, and running development servers.

5. **Node.js and npm (Node Package Manager)**: If you plan to work with JavaScript libraries, frameworks, or build tools, Node.js and npm are essential. Node.js allows you to run JavaScript on the server, while npm provides a vast repository of JavaScript packages.

6. **Local Development Server**: For testing and previewing web projects locally, consider using a local development server. Tools like Live Server for Visual Studio Code or webpack-dev-server provide live reloading and other features to streamline development.

7. **Graphics Software**: Depending on your projects, you might need graphics software like Adobe Photoshop or GIMP for image editing and optimization.

8. **Cloud Services**: Explore cloud services like AWS, Azure, or Netlify for deploying web applications and hosting your projects.

Platform Considerations

Your choice of operating system is a matter of personal preference and project requirements. Web development can be done effectively on Windows, macOS, or Linux. Some tools and software might be more readily available or optimized for one platform, so choose the one that aligns with your needs.

Workspace Customization

Your development environment should reflect your unique workflow and preferences. Spend some time customizing your text editor or IDE by installing extensions, themes, and keybindings that enhance your productivity and comfort.

Ready to Dive In

With your development environment set up and tailored to your liking, you're now prepared to dive headfirst into the world of web development. In the chapters that follow, we'll explore HTML, CSS, and JavaScript in depth, uncovering the secrets of crafting web experiences that captivate, inform, and inspire. Whether you're a seasoned developer or just starting your journey, your development environment is the springboard to a world of endless possibilities in web development. So, let's get started!

Chapter 1: HTML Fundamentals

1.1 Understanding HTML Syntax

HTML, or Hypertext Markup Language, is the backbone of the web. It's the language that allows us to structure content, define elements, and create the building blocks of every web page you've ever visited. In this section, we'll dive deep into understanding HTML syntax—the set of rules that govern how we write HTML code.

1.1.1 The Language of Structured Content

Imagine HTML as the structural blueprint of a web page. Just as architects use plans to build a house, web developers use

HTML to define the structure of a web document. HTML uses a system of tags, elements, and attributes to accomplish this.

1.1.2 HTML Tags and Elements

HTML uses tags to define elements on a webpage. Tags are enclosed in angle brackets, like <tagname>. An element consists of an opening tag, content, and a closing tag. For example:

```
<p>This is a paragraph.</p>
```

- <p> is the opening tag.
- This is a paragraph. is the content.
- </p> is the closing tag.

Elements can be nested within one another to create a hierarchical structure. Understanding this structure is key to creating well-organized web content.

1.1.3 HTML Document Structure

Every HTML document follows a basic structure:

```
<!DOCTYPE html>

<html>

    <head>

        <meta charset="UTF-8">

        <title>Document Title</title>

    </head>
```

```
<body>

    <!-- Content goes here -->

</body>

</html>
```

- `<!DOCTYPE html>` defines the document type and version.
- `<html>` is the root element that wraps the entire document.
- `<head>` contains metadata, such as the document title and character encoding.
- `<body>` holds the visible content of the web page.

1.1.4 HTML Attributes

HTML elements can have attributes that provide additional information about them. Attributes are always specified in the opening tag and follow this format: `attribute="value"`. For instance:

```
<a href="https://www.example.com">Visit Example</a>
```

In this example, `href` is the attribute, and `"https://www.example.com"` is the attribute value. Attributes vary depending on the element and can modify their behavior or appearance.

1.1.5 Void Elements

Some HTML elements are void elements, meaning they don't have a closing tag. Instead, they self-close using a forward slash, like `<img>`, `<br>`, or `<input>`. For example:

```
<img src="image.jpg" alt="An image">
```

1.1.6 HTML Comments

HTML allows you to insert comments within your code for documentation or clarification. Comments are ignored by browsers and are written as:

```
<!-- This is a comment -->
```

Comments are valuable for annotating your code and explaining its purpose to yourself and others.

1.1.7 Validating HTML

To ensure that your HTML code is correctly structured, you can use online validation tools like the W3C Markup Validation Service. These tools can help you catch syntax errors and ensure your code adheres to web standards.

In this section, we've laid the foundation for understanding HTML syntax—the rules and conventions that govern the structure of web documents. As we delve deeper into HTML fundamentals, we'll explore how to create diverse content, from headings and paragraphs to lists and hyperlinks, enriching our understanding of this fundamental web development language.

1.2 Working with Headings, Paragraphs, and Text Formatting

In the previous section, we explored the basic syntax of HTML, the language that structures the content of web pages. In this section, we'll delve deeper into the world of content creation by learning how to use headings, paragraphs, and text formatting to convey information effectively.

1.2.1 Organizing Content with Headings

Headings are fundamental elements for structuring content hierarchically. HTML provides six levels of headings, from <h1> (the highest) to <h6> (the lowest). These tags are used to define headings and subheadings within your content.

```
<h1>This is a Level 1 Heading</h1>

<h2>This is a Level 2 Heading</h2>

<h3>This is a Level 3 Heading</h3>
```

Using headings appropriately helps both users and search engines understand the organization and importance of your content. <h1> is typically used for the main title or heading of a page, while <h2> through <h6> are used for subsections.

1.2.2 Creating Paragraphs

Paragraphs, defined by the <p> tag, are the primary means of structuring textual content within an HTML document. They provide a clear separation between distinct blocks of text.

```
<p>This is a paragraph of text. It can
contain <em>emphasized</em> and
<strong>strongly emphasized</strong>
text.</p>
```

In addition to regular text, paragraphs can include inline elements for text formatting, as demonstrated with `<em>` (emphasis) and `<strong>` (strong emphasis) tags in the example above.

1.2.3 Text Formatting

HTML offers a range of tags for text formatting, enabling you to emphasize, highlight, or differentiate specific portions of your content:

- `<em>` (Emphasis): Italicizes text to indicate emphasis.
- `<strong>` (Strong Emphasis): Bolds text for strong emphasis or importance.
- `<mark>` (Marked Text): Highlights text to draw attention to it.
- `<del>` (Deleted Text): Strikes through text to indicate that it has been removed.
- `<ins>` (Inserted Text): Underlines text to indicate that it has been added.
- `<sub>` (Subscript): Renders text as a subscript (e.g., H₂O).
- `<sup>` (Superscript): Renders text as a superscript (e.g., x²).

```
<p>HTML provides various text formatting
options. For example, you can
<em>emphasize</em> important points,
<strong>highlight</strong> critical
information, or <mark>mark</mark>
significant content.</p>
```

1.2.4 Line Breaks and Horizontal Rules

To control line breaks within your content, you can use the
`<br>` tag. This tag inserts a line break without starting a new
paragraph.

```
<p>This is the first line.<br>This is the
second line.</p>
```

To create horizontal lines that visually separate content
sections, you can use the `<hr>` tag.

1.2.5 Special Characters

In HTML, some characters have special meanings and cannot
be used directly in your content. To display these characters,
you should use character entities, which start with an
ampersand (`&`) and end with a semicolon (`;`). For example,
`&lt;` represents <, and `&amp;` represents &.

```
<p>Use &lt;p&gt; to create paragraphs in
HTML.</p>
```

Understanding how to work with headings, paragraphs, and
text formatting is essential for crafting well-structured and
readable web content. In the next section, we'll explore lists

and tables, which provide another way to organize and present information on your web pages.

1.3 Creating Lists and Tables

In our journey through HTML fundamentals, we've already explored the essentials of structuring content, working with headings, paragraphs, and text formatting. Now, let's expand our toolkit by learning how to create lists and tables—powerful tools for organizing and presenting information on web pages.

1.3.1 Organizing Content with Lists

Lists are invaluable for organizing information in a structured and easily digestible manner. HTML offers three main types of lists: unordered lists, ordered lists, and definition lists.

1.3.1.1 Unordered Lists (<ul>)

Unordered lists are used to present items in a bulleted or unordered fashion. Each item is defined using the <li> (list item) tag.

```
<ul>
    <li>Item 1</li>
    <li>Item 2</li>
    <li>Item 3</li>
</ul>
```

This code generates a simple bulleted list:

- Item 1
- Item 2
- Item 3

1.3.1.2 Ordered Lists (`<ol>`)

Ordered lists are used to present items in a numbered or ordered sequence. Like unordered lists, each item is defined with the `<li>` tag.

```
<ol>
    <li>First item</li>
    <li>Second item</li>
    <li>Third item</li>
</ol>
```

This code creates a numbered list:

1. First item
2. Second item
3. Third item

1.3.1.3 Definition Lists (`<dl>`)

Definition lists are ideal for defining terms or glossary-like content. They consist of `<dt>` (definition term) for the term itself and `<dd>` (definition description) for the description.

```
<dl>
    <dt>HTML</dt>
    <dd>Hypertext Markup Language</dd>
    <dt>CSS</dt>
    <dd>Cascading Style Sheets</dd>
</dl>
```

This code produces a definition list:

- **HTML**
  - Hypertext Markup Language

- **CSS**
  - Cascading Style Sheets

1.3.2 Creating Tables (`<table>`)

Tables are a robust way to organize data into rows and columns, making them highly suitable for presenting structured information. HTML tables are created using the `<table>` element.

```
<table>
    <tr>
        <th>Header 1</th>
        <th>Header 2</th>
    </tr>
    <tr>
        <td>Data 1</td>
        <td>Data 2</td>
    </tr>
    <tr>
        <td>Data 3</td>
        <td>Data 4</td>
    </tr>
</table>
```

- `<table>` defines the table.
- `<tr>` represents table rows.
- `<th>` is used for table headers (typically bold and centered).
- `<td>` represents table data cells.

This code generates a simple table:

Header 1	Header 2
Data 1	Data 2
Data 3	Data 4

1.3.3 Semantic HTML Elements

In modern web development, it's important to use semantic HTML elements that convey the meaning and purpose of the content. Semantic elements like `<ul>`, `<ol>`, `<table>`, and their associated tags provide clarity and accessibility, helping both humans and search engines understand your content.

1.3.4 Styling Lists and Tables

While HTML defines the structure of lists and tables, CSS is used to control their appearance. You can apply styles to lists and tables to make them visually appealing and in line with your website's design.

In this section, we've explored the art of creating lists and tables in HTML, two essential tools for organizing and presenting information on web pages. In the next chapter, we'll journey into the world of forms, where we'll learn how to collect data from users and create interactive web experiences.

1.4 Forms and Input Elements

As we continue our exploration of HTML fundamentals, we venture into the realm of forms and input elements. Forms are crucial components of web development, allowing us to collect user data, facilitate interactions, and create dynamic web experiences. In this section, we'll unravel the power of forms and their associated input elements.

1.4.1 The Role of Forms

Forms are the digital equivalent of paper forms, providing a structured way for users to input and submit data to web applications. Whether it's signing up for a newsletter, completing a survey, or making an online purchase, forms enable user interactions that drive the functionality of countless websites and applications.

1.4.2 Creating a Form (`<form>`)

To create a form, you use the `<form>` element. This element acts as a container for various input elements, defining where the user's data will be submitted.

```
<form action="/submit" method="post">
    <!-- Input elements go here -->
</form>
```

- `action` specifies the URL where the form data will be sent.

- `method` defines the HTTP method for sending data (usually "GET" or "POST").

1.4.3 Common Input Elements

Input elements come in various types, each tailored to collect specific types of data. Here are some common input types:

31

- **Text Input** (`<input type="text">`): Used for single-line text input, such as names and email addresses.

```
<label for="name">Name:</label>

<input type="text" id="name"
name="name">
```

- **Password Input** (`<input type="password">`): Conceals the entered text, often used for password fields.

```
<label
for="password">Password:</label>
<input type="password" id="password"
name="password">
```

- **Radio Buttons** (`<input type="radio">`): Allow users to select a single option from a list.

```
<label for="male">Male</label>
<input type="radio" id="male"
name="gender" value="male"> <label
for="female">Female</label>
<input type="radio" id="female"
name="gender" value="female">
```

- **Checkboxes** (`<input type="checkbox">`): Permit users to select multiple options.

```
<label for="subscribe">Subscribe to
Newsletter</label> <input
```

```
type="checkbox" id="subscribe"
name="subscribe">
```

- **Select Dropdown** (`<select>`): Presents a dropdown list for users to select from.

```
<label for="country">Country:</label>
<select id="country" name="country">
    <option value="usa">USA</option>
    <option
value="canada">Canada</option>
    <!-- More options... -->
</select>
```

- **Textarea** (`<textarea>`): Provides a multi-line text input area, suitable for longer responses.

```
<label
for="comments">Comments:</label>
<textarea id="comments"
name="comments" rows="4"
cols="50"></textarea>
```

1.4.4 Form Controls and Attributes

- `<label>` **Element:** Labels are used to provide context and improve accessibility for form controls. They are linked to input elements using the `for` attribute.

```
<label for="name">Name:</label>
<input type="text" id="name"
name="name">
```

- name **Attribute:** The name attribute associates input elements with the data they represent. When the form is submitted, the name attribute is used as the field name in the submitted data.

1.4.5 Submitting and Resetting a Form

To allow users to submit the form, you can use the `<input type="submit">` button. Additionally, the `<input type="reset">` button resets the form to its initial state, clearing user input.

```
<input type="submit" value="Submit">
<input type="reset" value="Reset">
```

1.4.6 Form Validation

Form validation ensures that user input meets specified criteria before submission. HTML5 introduced built-in validation attributes, such as `required` and `pattern`, to streamline this process.

```
<input type="text" id="email" name="email"
required pattern="[a-z0-9._%+-]+@[a-z0-
9.-]+\.[a-z]{2,}$">
```

In this section, we've scratched the surface of creating forms and input elements in HTML. Forms are powerful tools for collecting user data and enabling interactions on web pages. As you progress in your web development journey, you'll explore more advanced form features and learn to enhance form functionality using JavaScript. In the upcoming sections, we'll continue our exploration of HTML fundamentals, delving into more aspects of web development with HTML, CSS, and JavaScript.

1.5 Semantic HTML for Accessibility

In our journey through HTML fundamentals, we've explored the core concepts of structuring content, working with headings, paragraphs, text formatting, creating lists and tables, and building forms with input elements. Now, we turn our attention to a critical aspect of web development—semantic HTML for accessibility.

1.5.1 The Significance of Semantic HTML

Semantic HTML, often referred to as "meaningful HTML," involves using HTML elements that convey the meaning and purpose of the content they contain. This practice not only enhances the understandability of your web documents by humans but is also a cornerstone of web accessibility.

1.5.2 Benefits of Semantic HTML for Accessibility

Semantic HTML provides several key benefits for web accessibility:

- **Improved Screen Reader Compatibility:** Screen readers are assistive technologies used by individuals with visual impairments. Semantic HTML ensures that screen readers can interpret and present content accurately, making your website accessible to a wider audience.

- **Enhanced Keyboard Navigation:** Semantic elements, like headings and lists, allow keyboard users to navigate your content efficiently. This is crucial for users who cannot rely on a mouse or other pointing devices.

- **Structured Content:** Semantic HTML helps organize content hierarchically, making it easier for all users to understand the relationships between different sections of your web page.

5.3 Key Semantic HTML Elements

Here are some essential semantic HTML elements and their roles:

- `<header>`: Represents the introductory content or a container for a group of introductory content. It often includes the website's logo, navigation, or headings.

- `<nav>`: Defines a section of navigation links, such as a menu bar or a list of links to other pages.

- `<main>`: Signifies the main content of the document, excluding headers, footers, or sidebars.

- `<article>`: Encloses a self-contained composition in a document, such as a news article, blog post, or forum post.

- `<section>`: Divides content into sections, often with its own heading. It is used to structure content within an `<article>` or `<main>`.

- `<aside>`: Represents content tangentially related to the content around it, like sidebars, pull quotes, or advertisements.

- `<footer>`: Contains footer information for a section or the document as a whole. It can include copyright notices, contact information, or related links.

1.5.4 Using Semantic Elements

To apply semantic HTML, choose the appropriate element for your content's purpose. For instance, if you have a navigation menu, wrap it in a `<nav>` element. If you have an article, use the `<article>` element. Here's an example:

```
<article>
  <h2>Web Accessibility Best Practices</h2>
  <p>Web accessibility is crucial for...</p>
</article>
```

In this example, the `<article>` element semantically encapsulates the article content, and the `<h2>` heading signifies the title of the article.

1.5.5 Additional Accessibility Considerations

In addition to using semantic HTML elements, consider other accessibility practices, such as providing descriptive text for images using the `alt` attribute, ensuring proper contrast between text and background colors, and testing your website with accessibility tools to identify and address potential issues.

By embracing semantic HTML and adopting accessibility best practices, you not only create a web environment that is inclusive and user-friendly but also position yourself as a responsible and conscientious web developer. In the upcoming sections of this book, we'll delve further into web development with HTML, CSS, and JavaScript, exploring advanced topics and techniques to create web experiences that are not only visually appealing but also accessible to all.

Chapter 2: CSS Styling Basics

Welcome to the world of cascading style sheets, or CSS—a pivotal component in the art of web development. In this chapter, we will embark on a journey to unravel the mysteries of CSS, empowering you to craft captivating and visually appealing web experiences.

Cascading Style Sheets (CSS) serve as the design and presentation layer of web development. HTML provides the structure and content of a web page, while CSS steps in to control the layout, formatting, and visual styling. It's the painter's palette, the wardrobe stylist's closet, and the interior decorator's toolkit of the web world—all rolled into one.

CSS employs a simple yet powerful syntax that revolves around selectors, properties, and values. Together, they form rules that dictate how HTML elements should be styled. Here's a glimpse of the CSS syntax:

```
selector {

  property: value;

}
```

- **Selector:** Identifies which HTML elements the rule should apply to. Selectors can target specific elements, classes, IDs, or even complex patterns.

- **Property:** Specifies the aspect of the element to be styled, such as `color`, `font-size`, `margin`, or `background-color`.

- **Value:** Sets the desired style for the property. For example, `red` for color or `16px` for font size.

CSS styles can be applied to HTML elements in several ways:

- **Inline Styles:** Placing styles directly within the HTML element using the `style` attribute.

  ```
  <p style="color: blue;">This is a blue
  paragraph.</p>
  ```

- **Internal Styles:** Defining styles within a `<style>` block in the `<head>` section of an HTML document.

```
<head>
    <style>
        p {
            color: green;
        }
    </style>
</head>
<body>
    <p>This is a green paragraph.</p>
</body>
```

- **External Stylesheets:** Creating a separate CSS file and linking it to your HTML document using the `<link>` element.

The term "cascading" in CSS refers to the order of priority and inheritance when multiple styles conflict or overlap. CSS rules are applied following a specific hierarchy:

1. **User Agent Styles:** These are the default styles applied by web browsers.

2. **Author Styles:** These are the styles defined by the web developer in the CSS.

3. **User Styles:** Styles that users can apply to override author styles.

4. **!important:** Styles marked with `!important` have the highest priority.

5. **Specificity:** More specific selectors override less specific ones.

6. **Order of Appearance:** Styles defined later in the CSS file override earlier ones.

2.1 Selectors, Properties and Values

In the world of web development, Cascading Style Sheets (CSS) are the magic wand that transforms the bland into the beautiful. To master CSS, we need to understand its fundamental building blocks: **selectors**, **properties**, and **values**. These elements, combined with the CSS syntax we discussed earlier, enable us to breathe life into our web designs.

2.1.1 Selectors: Targeting the Elements

Think of selectors as the precision tools in your CSS toolkit. They determine which HTML elements your styles will apply to. CSS provides a variety of selectors to choose from:

1. **Element Selectors:** These are the simplest and most common selectors. You target specific HTML elements by using their tag name. For example, p targets all paragraphs, while h1 targets all top-level headings.

2. **Class Selectors:** Classes are reusable and versatile. You assign a class to one or more elements using the class attribute in HTML, and then you target those elements in your CSS using a period (.) followed by the class name. For instance, if you have <div class="box">, you can select it with .box in your CSS.

3. **ID Selectors:** IDs are unique and should only be assigned to a single element on a page. You use the `id` attribute in HTML to set an ID, and in CSS, you target it using a hash (#) followed by the ID name. For example, `<div id="header">` can be selected with `#header` in CSS.

4. **Descendant Selectors:** These selectors allow you to target elements that are descendants of another element. For instance, `ul li` selects all list items within unordered lists.

5. **Pseudo-Classes and Pseudo-Elements:** Pseudo-classes, like `:hover` or `:focus`, enable you to style elements based on their state or interaction. Pseudo-elements, such as `::before` or `::after`, let you style parts of an element.

6. **Attribute Selectors:** You can select elements based on their attributes. For instance, `[type="text"]` selects all input elements with `type="text"`.

2.1.2 Properties: Defining the Styles

Once you've targeted your elements using selectors, it's time to define their styles using properties. Properties are like the adjectives in your CSS language; they describe how elements should appear or behave. Here are some common CSS properties:

- `color`: Sets the text color.

- `background-color`: Defines the background color.

- `font-family`: Specifies the font to be used for text.

- `font-size`: Sets the size of the font.

- `margin` **and** `padding`: Control spacing around elements.

- `border`: Defines the border of an element.

- `width` **and** `height`: Determine the dimensions of elements.

- `display`: Specifies how an element should be displayed, such as `block`, `inline`, or `none`.

- `position`: Defines the positioning method for an element, such as `relative`, `absolute`, or `fixed`.

2.1.3 Values: Fine-Tuning the Style

Properties are nothing without values; they work together to bring your designs to life. Values are the specific settings you apply to properties. For example:

- For `color`, you might use values like `red`, `#00ff00` (hex color code), or `rgba(255, 0, 0, 0.5)` (RGBA color with alpha transparency).

- For `font-size`, you can use values like `16px`, `2rem` (relative to the root font size), or `100%` (relative to the parent element's font size).

44

- For `margin`, you could set values like `10px` (equal margin on all sides), `5px 10px` (top and bottom 5px, left and right 10px), or `0` (no margin).

Values provide fine-grained control over how your styles are applied. They can be absolute units like pixels (`px`) or relative units like percentages (`%`) and ems (`em`).

By understanding how selectors, properties, and values interact, you can craft precise and visually appealing styles for your web pages. In the chapters that follow, we'll dive deeper into the art of CSS, exploring more advanced techniques, layout strategies, positioning and floating, and responsive design principles to elevate your web development skills to new heights.

2.2 Text Styling and Formatting

Text is the backbone of web content, and the way it's presented can greatly impact the readability and aesthetics of a website. In this section, we'll delve into CSS text styling and formatting, equipping you with the tools to make your text visually appealing and accessible.

2.2.1 Font Properties: The Typography of Text

CSS provides a range of font properties to control the typography of your text:

- `font-family`: Specifies the typeface or font family to be used. You can list multiple font names to provide fallback options.

- `font-size`: Determines the size of the font, which can be specified in various units such as pixels (`px`), ems (`em`), percentages (`%`), or keywords (`medium`, `large`, `small`).

- `font-weight`: Adjusts the thickness or boldness of the font. You can use values like `normal`, `bold`, or numeric values ranging from `100` to `900`.

- `font-style`: Sets the style of the font, allowing you to choose between `normal`, `italic`, or `oblique`.

- `text-transform`: Modifies the capitalization of text, transforming it to `uppercase`, `lowercase`, or `capitalize` the first letter of each word.

2.2.2 Text Color and Background

- `color`: Defines the color of the text using keywords, hexadecimal codes, RGB or RGBA values.

- `background-color`: Sets the background color behind the text, making it visually distinct from the surrounding content.

2.2.3 Text Alignment

- `text-align`: Controls the horizontal alignment of text within its container. You can use values like `left`, `right`, `center`, or `justify`.

2.2.4 Text Decoration

- `text-decoration`: Adds visual decorations to text, such as `underline`, `overline`, `line-through`, or `none` for no decoration.

2.2.5 Line Height and Spacing

- `line-height`: Sets the height of a line of text, affecting the vertical spacing between lines. It's often used to improve readability and aesthetics.

- `letter-spacing`: Adjusts the space between characters, useful for fine-tuning the overall text appearance.

2.2.6 Text Shadow

- `text-shadow`: Creates a shadow effect behind the text. You can specify the shadow's color, horizontal offset, vertical offset, and blur radius.

2.2.7 Word Wrapping and Overflow

- `word-wrap`: Controls how long words or strings of characters are broken to fit within the container. Values like `normal` and `break-word` are commonly used.

- `overflow`: Determines how text that overflows its container should be handled, with options like `hidden`, `scroll`, or `auto`.

2.2.8 Text Indentation and Alignment

- `text-indent`: Sets the indentation of the first line of text within an element, creating a visually pleasing layout.

- `text-align-last`: Specifies the alignment of the last line of text within a block container.

2.2.9 Text Transformation and Spacing

- `text-transform`: Alters the capitalization of text, making it uppercase, lowercase, or capitalized.

- `white-space`: Controls how whitespace inside an element is handled, influencing text wrapping and spacing.

By skillfully using these CSS properties, you can finely craft the appearance of text on your web pages, ensuring that it not only looks great but also enhances readability and user experience.

2.3 Box Model and Layout

The Box Model is a fundamental concept in CSS that governs how elements are structured and sized on a web page. Understanding the Box Model and mastering layout techniques are crucial steps in crafting well-structured and visually appealing web designs.

2.3.1 The Box Model

At its core, the Box Model conceptualizes every HTML element as a rectangular box. This box is composed of four crucial components:

- **Content:** The innermost part of the box that holds the actual content, such as text or images.

- **Padding:** The space between the content and the element's border. It provides breathing room within the box.

- **Border:** A line that surrounds the padding and content, serving as a visual and structural boundary.

- **Margin:** The outermost space, which separates the element from neighboring elements. Margins are used for layout and spacing.

When you apply styles to an element, you often set properties like `width`, `height`, `padding`, `border`, and `margin`. These properties collectively determine the size and spacing of the box.

2.3.2 Box Model Properties

- `width` **and** `height`: These properties set the dimensions of the content box. You can specify values in pixels (`px`), percentages (`%`), ems (`em`), or other units.

- `padding`: Defines the space between the content and the element's border. You can set padding for individual sides (e.g., `padding-left`, `padding-top`) or use shorthand notation (e.g., `padding: 10px 20px 15px 5px;`).

- `border`: Specifies the border around the element. You can control the border's width, style, and color. For example, `border: 1px solid #000;` creates a 1-pixel solid black border.

- `margin`: Sets the space outside the element, affecting its positioning relative to other elements. Like padding, you can set margins for individual sides or use shorthand notation.

2.3.3 Layout Techniques

Mastering layout techniques in CSS is essential for creating responsive and visually appealing web designs. Here are some key layout concepts:

- **Block-level vs. Inline Elements:** Elements can be block-level (e.g., `<div>`, `<p>`) or inline (e.g.,

`<span>`, `<a>`). Block-level elements create a new block formatting context and stack vertically, while inline elements flow within the content.

- **Display Property:** The `display` property allows you to change how elements behave in terms of layout. For instance, you can use `display: inline-block;` to make an element flow like an inline element but retain block-level properties like setting dimensions.

- **Floats:** The `float` property enables elements to float left or right within their parent container, which is useful for creating text wraps around images or creating complex multi-column layouts.

- **Positioning:** CSS offers several positioning options, including `relative`, `absolute`, `fixed`, and `sticky`. These properties are essential for precise control over element placement.

- **Flexbox:** Flexbox is a powerful layout system that simplifies complex layouts by providing a flexible way to distribute space and align content within a container. It's particularly useful for creating responsive designs.

- **Grid:** CSS Grid Layout is another advanced layout system that offers precise control over both row and column layouts. It's well-suited for creating grid-based designs.

- **Responsive Design:** With media queries and relative units like percentages and ems, you can create responsive layouts that adapt to different screen sizes and orientations.

By understanding the Box Model and mastering layout techniques, you'll have the foundation to craft visually appealing, well-structured, and responsive web designs.

2.4 CSS Positioning and Floating

CSS positioning and floating are essential techniques that give you precise control over the placement and arrangement of elements on your web page. In this section, we'll explore these techniques, allowing you to create complex layouts and achieve the desired design for your website.

2.4.1 CSS Positioning

CSS positioning enables you to control the exact position of an element on a web page. There are several positioning values you can use:

- `static`: This is the default value. Elements with `position: static;` are placed in the normal flow of the document and are not affected by top, bottom, left, or right properties.

- `relative`: When you set `position: relative;`, you can use `top`, `bottom`, `left`, or `right` properties to shift the element's position relative to where it would have been in the normal flow.

- `absolute`: Elements with `position: absolute;` are removed from the normal document flow and positioned relative to their nearest positioned ancestor (or the initial containing block if none is found). This allows you to precisely place elements anywhere on the page.

- `fixed`: Similar to `absolute`, elements with `position: fixed;` are removed from the document flow and positioned relative to the viewport. This means they stay in the same position even when the page is scrolled.

- `sticky`: Sticky positioning combines aspects of both `relative` and `fixed`. An element with `position: sticky;` is initially in the normal flow but becomes `fixed` once it reaches a defined scroll position.

2.4.2 CSS Floating

CSS floating is a layout technique used to wrap text around images or other elements. It's particularly handy for creating multi-column layouts and designing magazine-style web pages. Elements can be floated to the left or right within their containing element.

To apply floating:

- Use the `float` property with values like `left` or `right`. For example, `float: left;` will float an element to the left, allowing content to flow around it.

- After floating an element, you may need to clear the float to ensure that subsequent content is not affected. This is often done using the `clear` property. For instance, `clear: both;` clears both left and right floats.

2.4.3 Practical Use Cases

CSS positioning and floating can be used for various purposes:

- Creating multi-column layouts by floating divs or other container elements.

- Designing navigation menus that stay fixed at the top of the page as users scroll (using `position: fixed;`).

- Building complex forms or image galleries where elements need precise placement (using `position: absolute;`).

- Wrapping text around images or infographics (using `float`).

- Implementing sticky headers or sidebars (using `position: sticky;`).

2.4.4 Caveats and Considerations

While CSS positioning and floating are powerful tools, they can also introduce challenges, such as clearing floats, managing layout responsiveness, and handling overlap or z-index issues.

Additionally, modern layout techniques like Flexbox and CSS Grid are often preferred for more complex layouts due to their ease of use and better support for responsive design. These techniques should be explored as you advance in your web development journey.

By mastering CSS positioning and floating, you'll have a solid foundation for controlling the layout of your web pages. As you progress through this book, you'll explore advanced layout techniques and responsive design principles that build upon these fundamental concepts, enabling you to create stunning and functional web layouts.

2.5 Responsive Web Design with Media Queries

In today's diverse landscape of devices and screen sizes, responsive web design has become a fundamental skill for web developers. The ability to create websites that adapt gracefully to various viewport sizes is crucial for delivering an optimal user experience. This section introduces the concept of responsive web design using media queries.

2.5.1 Understanding Media Queries

A **media query** is a CSS technique that allows you to apply different styles based on the characteristics of the user's device or viewport. By examining factors like screen width, height, orientation, and resolution, you can tailor your design to suit a wide range of devices, from large desktop monitors to small smartphones.

Media queries are written using the `@media` rule in CSS and typically follow this structure:

```
@media screen and (max-width: 768px) {
    /* CSS rules for screens with a maximum width
of 768px */
}
```

In the example above, the CSS rules within the media query block will only apply when the screen width is 768 pixels or less. You can use various operators such as `min-width`, `max-width`, `orientation`, and others to target specific conditions.

2.5.2 Creating Responsive Layouts

Media queries are often used to adapt the layout of a web page for different screen sizes. Here are some common techniques:

- **Adjusting Typography:** You can change font sizes, line heights, and margins to ensure text remains readable on small screens while optimizing it for larger displays.

- **Changing Layouts:** Modify the layout by adjusting the widths, positioning, and spacing of elements. For example, you might switch from a multi-column to a single-column layout on smaller screens.

- **Hiding or Showing Content:** Hide or display certain elements based on screen size. This is useful for showing or hiding navigation menus, sidebars, or non-essential content on smaller screens.

2.5.3 Retina and High-Resolution Displays

Some devices, like Retina displays, have higher pixel densities, which can affect image quality. Media queries can also be used to serve higher resolution images to such devices. For example:

```
@media screen and (-webkit-min-device-pixel-ratio:
2), (min-resolution: 192dpi) {
    /* CSS rules for high-resolution displays */
}
```

2.5.4 Testing and Debugging

To effectively implement responsive web design, it's crucial to test your website on various devices and screen sizes. You can use browser developer tools to simulate different viewport sizes and orientations. Additionally, there are online testing tools and services that can help ensure your design looks great on a wide range of devices.

2.5.5 Frameworks and Libraries

Many front-end frameworks and libraries, such as Bootstrap and Foundation, come with responsive design built-in. They provide pre-designed responsive grids, components, and styles, making it easier to create responsive websites without starting from scratch.

2.5.6 Best Practices

Responsive web design is not just about accommodating different screen sizes; it's also about delivering a consistent and user-friendly experience. Here are some best practices:

- Prioritize content: Make sure essential content is visible and accessible on all devices.

- Optimize images: Use responsive images and consider using the `srcset` attribute to provide different image resolutions.

- Test thoroughly: Continuously test your website on various devices and browsers to ensure a seamless user experience.

Responsive web design is an essential skill for modern web developers. By mastering media queries and responsive design principles, you'll be well-equipped to create websites that provide an excellent user experience across a wide range of devices and screen sizes. As you progress in your web development journey, you'll dive deeper into advanced techniques for responsive layouts and interactivity.

Chapter 3: Advanced CSS Techniques

3.1 Mastering Flexbox Layout

In the ever-evolving world of web development, achieving complex layouts and arranging elements consistently across various screen sizes has been a historical challenge. Enter Flexbox, a revolutionary CSS layout model that simplifies the process of creating flexible and responsive designs. In this section, we'll delve into Flexbox layout, exploring its principles, properties, and practical applications.

3.1.1 Understanding Flexbox

Flexbox, short for Flexible Box Layout, is a one-dimensional layout model. It focuses on distributing space along a single axis—either horizontally or vertically—within a container. This approach makes it ideal for creating both simple and intricate layouts with ease.

3.1.2 Key Concepts of Flexbox

To master Flexbox, you need to grasp some fundamental concepts:

- **Flex Container:** This is the parent element that contains the flex items. You apply the `display: flex;` property to create a flex container.

- **Flex Items:** These are the child elements of the flex container. By default, they align horizontally (in a row), but you can adjust this by using the `flex-direction` property.

- **Main Axis:** The primary axis along which flex items are distributed. It can be horizontal (`row`) or vertical (`column`).

- **Cross Axis:** The perpendicular axis to the main axis. If the main axis is horizontal, the cross axis is vertical, and vice versa.

3.1.3 Flex Container Properties

Flex containers are governed by several properties that enable you to control layout and alignment:

- `display`: Set to `flex` to create a flex container.

- `flex-direction`: Determines the direction of the main axis. Options include `row`, `row-reverse`, `column`, and `column-reverse`.

- `justify-content`: Controls how flex items are distributed along the main axis. You can use values like `flex-start`, `flex-end`, `center`, `space-between`, and `space-around`.

- `align-items`: Defines how flex items are aligned along the cross axis. Options include `flex-start`, `flex-end`, `center`, `baseline`, and `stretch`.

- `flex-wrap`: Specifies whether flex items should wrap onto a new line when they exceed the width (or height) of the flex container.

3.1.4 Flex Item Properties

Each flex item can have its own properties to control its behavior:

- `flex-grow`: Determines how much a flex item can grow relative to other items when there's extra space along the main axis.

- `flex-shrink`: Specifies how much a flex item can shrink when there's not enough space along the main axis.

- `flex-basis`: Sets the initial size of a flex item before it expands or shrinks.

- `order`: Assigns a numerical value to determine the order in which flex items appear along the main axis.

3.1.5 Practical Applications

Flexbox can be used for a wide range of design scenarios, including:

- Creating navigation menus that adapt to various screen sizes.

- Designing responsive grids and card layouts.

- Building flexible and consistent form layouts.

- Aligning content vertically and horizontally within containers.

- Crafting complex and adaptive navigation bars and sidebars.

3.1.6 Flexbox vs. Grid Layout

While Flexbox is excellent for one-dimensional layouts, Grid Layout excels at two-dimensional layouts. You can use both together to create sophisticated designs. Flexbox is ideal for arranging elements in a row or column, while Grid Layout is perfect for creating grid-based structures.

3.1.7 Browser Support

Flexbox has excellent support in modern browsers. However, if you need to support older versions of Internet Explorer (IE), you may encounter some compatibility issues, so it's essential to test and provide fallbacks when necessary.

3.1.8 Best Practices

When working with Flexbox, keep these best practices in mind:

- Start with simple layouts and gradually build complexity.

- Experiment with different combinations of properties to achieve your desired design.

- Test your layout across various devices and browsers to ensure consistency.

Flexbox is a powerful tool in your CSS toolkit, enabling you to create flexible and responsive layouts with ease. By mastering Flexbox layout principles and properties, you'll be well-prepared to tackle a wide range of design challenges and deliver seamless user experiences on the web. As we progress through this book, we'll explore more advanced CSS techniques, including Grid Layout, transitions, and animations.

3.2 Embracing CSS Grid Layout

In the world of web design, achieving complex grid-based layouts has traditionally been a formidable task. Enter CSS Grid Layout, a groundbreaking CSS feature that simplifies the creation of intricate two-dimensional layouts. In this section, we'll explore CSS Grid Layout, uncover its principles, properties, and practical applications, and understand how it complements other layout models like Flexbox.

3.2.1 Understanding CSS Grid Layout

CSS Grid Layout, often referred to simply as Grid, is a two-dimensional layout model. Unlike Flexbox, which operates along a single axis (either horizontally or vertically), Grid allows you to define rows and columns, providing precise control over both dimensions within a container.

3.2.2 Key Concepts of CSS Grid

To harness the full potential of CSS Grid, it's essential to grasp some fundamental concepts:

- **Grid Container:** This is the parent element that holds the grid items. You apply the `display: grid;` property to create a grid container.

- **Grid Items:** These are the child elements of the grid container. Each item is placed within rows and columns defined by the grid.

- **Grid Lines:** These are horizontal and vertical lines that form the grid structure. They create rows and columns, and you can refer to them by index numbers.

- **Grid Tracks:** These are the spaces between grid lines, forming rows and columns.

3.2.3 Creating a Grid

To create a grid, you define its structure by specifying the number and size of rows and columns using properties like `grid-template-rows` and `grid-template-columns`. For example:

```
.grid-container {
    display: grid;
    grid-template-rows: 100px 200px;
    grid-template-columns: 1fr 2fr 1fr;
}
```

In this example, we have a grid container with two rows (100px and 200px tall) and three columns (1 fractional unit, 2 fractional units, and 1 fractional unit wide).

3.2.4 Placing Grid Items

Grid items are placed within the grid container using properties like `grid-row` and `grid-column`. You can define their starting and ending positions along both the row and column axes.

```
.grid-item {
    grid-row: 1 / 3; /* Starts at row 1 and spans 2
rows */
    grid-column: 2 / 4; /* Starts at column 2 and
spans 2 columns */
}
```

3.2.5 Auto-Placement and Grid Gaps

Grid can also automatically place items using properties like `grid-auto-rows`, `grid-auto-columns`, and `grid-auto-flow`. Additionally, you can define gaps between rows and columns with `grid-gap` or its individual properties (`grid-row-gap` and `grid-column-gap`).

3.2.6 Practical Applications

CSS Grid is incredibly versatile and can be used for various design scenarios, including:

- Designing responsive grids that adapt seamlessly to different screen sizes.

- Creating flexible and adaptive card layouts for content presentation.

- Building complex navigation menus, sidebars, and multi-column forms.

- Crafting magazine-style layouts with image and text integration.

67

3.2.7 Grid vs. Flexbox

Grid and Flexbox serve different layout purposes. While Grid excels at two-dimensional layouts like grids and tables, Flexbox is ideal for one-dimensional layouts like navigation menus and card layouts. Often, you'll use both Grid and Flexbox together to create sophisticated designs.

3.2.8 Browser Support

CSS Grid has excellent support in modern browsers, making it a reliable choice for contemporary web development projects. However, if you need to support older browsers, you might need to provide fallbacks or alternative layouts.

3.2.9 Best Practices

When working with CSS Grid, consider these best practices:

- Plan your grid structure and layout requirements before implementation.

- Experiment with different row and column sizing techniques to achieve your design goals.

- Use Grid's auto-placement features when dealing with dynamic content.

CSS Grid Layout is a powerful tool for creating complex and responsive grid-based layouts with ease. By mastering Grid's principles and properties, you'll gain the capability to tackle diverse design challenges and provide exceptional user experiences on the web. As we advance through this book, we'll explore more advanced CSS techniques, including transitions, animations, and responsive design strategies.

3.3 Adding Life with CSS Transitions and Animations

As web development continues to evolve, user experience has become paramount. Adding transitions and animations to your web projects can significantly enhance the visual appeal and interactivity of your designs. In this section, we'll explore CSS transitions and animations, unveiling the principles, properties, and practical applications of these dynamic techniques.

3.3.1 CSS Transitions

Understanding Transitions: CSS transitions allow smooth, gradual changes in CSS properties over a specified duration. These changes can occur when an element is hovered over, clicked, or otherwise interacted with. Transitions are a fantastic way to add subtle motion and interactivity to your web pages.

Transition Properties: To create a transition, you define which CSS properties should change and specify the transition's duration and timing function. For example:

```
.button {
    background-color: #3498db;
    color: #fff;
    transition-property: background-color, color;
    transition-duration: 0.3s;
    transition-timing-function: ease-in-out;
}
```

```
.button:hover {
    background-color: #e74c3c;
    color: #fff;
}
```

In this example, the button's background color and text color will smoothly transition to their new values when the button is hovered over. The transition takes 0.3 seconds and uses an ease-in-out timing function for a smooth effect.

3.3.2 CSS Animations

Understanding Animations: CSS animations offer more advanced and complex motion effects compared to transitions. Animations involve defining keyframes that specify how an element's style should change at various points during an animation's duration.

Animation Keyframes: To create an animation, you define keyframes using the @keyframes rule. Each keyframe specifies the style of the element at a particular point in time during the animation. For example:

```
@keyframes slide {
    0% {
        transform: translateX(0);
    }
    100% {
        transform: translateX(100%);
    }
}
```

This keyframe animation, named "slide," smoothly moves an element from its initial position (0% progress) to the right by 100% of its width (100% progress) along the X-axis.

Animation Properties: You can apply animations to elements using the `animation` property, which defines the animation's name, duration, timing function, delay, iteration count, and direction. For example:

```
.element {
    animation: slide 1s ease-in-out 0s infinite
alternate;
}
```

In this case, the "slide" animation is applied to the element, taking 1 second to complete, using an ease-in-out timing function, with no delay, infinitely repeating, and alternating directions.

3.3.3 Practical Applications

Transitions and animations can be used to enhance various aspects of your web design, including:

- Creating engaging hover effects for buttons, links, and images.

- Adding subtle transitions to navigation menus for better user feedback.

- Building interactive image galleries with zoom or slide-in effects.

- Designing attention-grabbing banners and call-to-action sections.

- Implementing loading spinners or progress bars for a smoother user experience.

3.3.4 Browser Support

Both transitions and animations enjoy excellent support in modern browsers, making them a reliable choice for enhancing your web projects. However, when dealing with older browsers, you may need to provide fallbacks or alternative styling to ensure a consistent user experience.

3.3.5 Best Practices

When working with transitions and animations, consider these best practices:

- Keep animations subtle and purposeful, avoiding excessive motion that could distract users.

- Test animations on various devices and screen sizes to ensure they function correctly and remain responsive.

- Pay attention to performance, as complex animations can impact page loading times. Use CSS properties like `will-change` to optimize animations.

Transitions and animations are powerful tools to breathe life into your web designs. By mastering these techniques and understanding when and how to use them effectively, you'll elevate your ability to create visually appealing and engaging user experiences. As we progress through this book, we'll explore more advanced CSS techniques, including custom fonts and icons and CSS preprocessors.

3.4 Elevating Design with Custom Fonts and Icons

In the realm of web design, typography and iconography play pivotal roles in shaping a website's identity and user experience. By harnessing custom fonts and icons, you can infuse creativity, uniqueness, and visual appeal into your web projects. In this section, we'll explore the use of custom fonts and icons in web development, understanding their importance and practical implementation.

3.4.1 Custom Fonts

Enhancing Typography: While web browsers provide a selection of default fonts, custom fonts allow you to break free from the confines of standard typography. Using custom fonts, you can establish a unique brand identity and enhance the readability and aesthetics of your website.

Font Formats: Custom fonts are typically provided in various formats, such as TrueType (.ttf), OpenType (.otf), Web Open Font Format (.woff), and Web Open Font Format 2 (.woff2). Each format is suited for specific use cases and browser compatibility.

Using @font-face: To include custom fonts in your web project, you can use the @font-face rule in CSS. This rule specifies the font family, sources for the font files, and fallback options. For example:

```
@font-face {
    font-family: 'CustomFont';
    src: url('custom-font.woff2') format('woff2'),
         url('custom-font.woff') format('woff');
}
```

Once defined, you can apply the custom font to specific elements using the font-family property:

```
body {
    font-family: 'CustomFont', sans-serif;
}
```

3.4.2 Icon Fonts

Solving Icon Challenges: Icons are essential for user interfaces, aiding in navigation, enhancing content, and conveying messages concisely. Icon fonts offer a scalable and efficient way to include icons in your web projects while overcoming challenges like resolution independence and ease of customization.

Icon Font Libraries: Several icon font libraries, such as Font Awesome, Material Icons, and Ionicons, provide a wide range of ready-to-use icons. These libraries simplify the integration of icons into your web designs.

Using Icon Fonts: To use an icon font, you include the font files in your project and apply the icons as pseudo-elements or inline elements in your HTML or CSS. For example:

```
<i class="icon icon-home"></i>

.icon::before {
    font-family: 'IconFont';
    content: '\e001'; /* Unicode character for the
home icon */
}
```

3.4.3 Practical Applications

Custom fonts and icon fonts can enhance your web design in various ways:

- **Branding:** Custom fonts can establish a unique brand identity and reinforce the design's personality.

- **Typography:** Custom fonts enable you to achieve specific typographic styles and layouts that aren't possible with default fonts.

- **Accessibility:** Icons can improve accessibility by providing visual cues and aiding navigation for users with disabilities.

- **Responsive Design:** Custom fonts and icon fonts can scale gracefully across different screen sizes and devices.

3.4.4 Browser Support

Custom fonts and icon fonts enjoy broad support in modern web browsers. However, to ensure compatibility with older browsers, you may need to provide fallback options or alternative styling.

3.4.5 Best Practices

Consider these best practices when using custom fonts and icon fonts:

- Optimize font loading for performance by using the `preload` attribute in HTML or the `font-display` property in CSS.

- Test your design on various devices and screen sizes to ensure fonts and icons render correctly.

- Comply with licensing agreements when using custom fonts, and be mindful of copyright and licensing issues with icon fonts.

Custom fonts and icon fonts are potent tools for elevating your web designs. By mastering their use and understanding the principles of typography and iconography, you'll be well-equipped to create visually compelling and unique user experiences. As we progress through this book, we'll explore more advanced CSS techniques like CSS preprocessors and best practices for CSS organization.

3.5 Streamlining CSS with Preprocessors (e.g., SASS)

As web development projects grow in complexity, managing and organizing your CSS code can become challenging. This is where CSS preprocessors like SASS (Syntactically Awesome Style Sheets) come into play. In this section, we'll explore the benefits of using CSS preprocessors and how they can streamline your CSS workflow.

3.5.1 What Are CSS Preprocessors?

CSS preprocessors are scripting languages that extend the capabilities of standard CSS. They introduce features like variables, nesting, functions, and mixins, which simplify the process of writing and maintaining CSS code. Preprocessors generate standard CSS files that can be used in web projects.

3.5.2 Advantages of CSS Preprocessors

Using a CSS preprocessor like SASS offers several advantages:

- **Variables:** You can define variables to store reusable values like colors, font sizes, or spacing. This promotes consistency and makes it easy to update styles globally.

- **Nesting:** Preprocessors allow you to nest CSS rules within one another, mirroring the structure of your

HTML markup. This improves readability and reduces redundancy.

- **Mixins:** Mixins are reusable blocks of CSS code that you can include in multiple rules. They are particularly useful for maintaining consistent styling patterns.

- **Functions:** Preprocessors introduce functions that enable you to perform calculations or manipulate values dynamically, such as generating gradients or scaling fonts based on viewport size.

- **Modularization:** CSS preprocessors facilitate breaking your styles into modular files, which can be imported and combined, making your codebase more organized and maintainable.

3.5.3 Using SASS as an Example

Let's take SASS as an example of a CSS preprocessor.

- **Installation:** You can install SASS on your development environment using npm (Node Package Manager) or other package managers.

- **SASS Syntax:** SASS offers two syntax options: SASS (indented syntax with no curly braces or semicolons) and SCSS (Sassy CSS, a syntax that closely resembles standard CSS). SCSS is more popular due to its familiarity.

- **Variables:**

```
$primary-color: #3498db;

.button {
    background-color: $primary-color;
}
```

- **Nesting:**

```
nav {
    ul {
        list-style-type: none;
        li {
            padding: 10px;
        }
    }
}
```

- **Mixins:**

```
@mixin border-radius($radius) {
    border-radius: $radius;
    -webkit-border-radius: $radius;
    -moz-border-radius: $radius;
}

.button {
    @include border-radius(5px);
}
```

3.5.4 Compiling SASS to CSS

Before using SASS in your web project, you need to compile it into standard CSS. This can be done using the SASS command-line tool or by using build tools like Gulp, Grunt, or Webpack. The compiled CSS files are what you include in your HTML documents.

79

3.5.5 Best Practices

- Keep your SASS code organized by using partials (files with underscores) to modularize styles.

- Comment your SASS code to provide context and explanations for future developers.

- Back up your SASS files regularly, as they serve as the source for generating CSS.

- Familiarize yourself with SASS documentation and best practices to make the most of its features.

CSS preprocessors like SASS can significantly improve the efficiency and maintainability of your CSS code. By incorporating variables, nesting, mixins, and other advanced features, you can streamline your CSS workflow, ensure consistency across your projects, and reduce the likelihood of errors.

3.6 Best Practices for CSS Organization

Effective CSS organization is crucial for maintaining and scaling your web development projects. As your stylesheets grow, adopting best practices becomes essential to ensure maintainability, readability, and collaboration among team members. In this section, we'll explore some best practices for organizing your CSS code.

3.6.1 Use a CSS Preprocessor

As mentioned earlier, using a CSS preprocessor like SASS or LESS can greatly enhance code organization. Preprocessors introduce features like variables, mixins, and nesting, which promote modularity and readability. This leads to cleaner and more maintainable CSS.

3.6.2 File Structure and Naming Conventions

A well-defined file structure and consistent naming conventions are essential for organizing your CSS. Here are some guidelines:

- **Folder Structure:** Divide your CSS files into logical folders, such as "base," "components," "layouts," and "utilities." This separation helps you find specific styles quickly.

- **File Naming:** Use descriptive and meaningful filenames. For example, instead of "style.css," consider naming your main stylesheet "main.css" or "app.css." Be consistent across your project.

3.6.3 Modularization with CSS Classes

Embrace modular CSS by using classes that encapsulate specific styles. This reduces the risk of global style conflicts and makes it easier to identify and update styles related to a particular component or element.

```
<div class="card">
    <h2 class="card-title">Article Title</h2>
```

81

```
    <p class="card-content">Lorem ipsum dolor sit
amet...</p>
</div>
```

In this example, the `.card` class encapsulates the styles for the card component.

3.6.4 BEM Methodology

Consider using a methodology like BEM (Block Element Modifier) for naming CSS classes. BEM promotes a consistent and readable class naming convention, which makes it easier to understand the structure and relationships between elements.

```
<div class="card">
    <h2 class="card__title">Article Title</h2>
    <p class="card__content">Lorem ipsum dolor sit
amet...</p>
</div>
```

In this BEM example, the class names follow a clear structure of `block__element--modifier`.

3.6.5 Comments and Documentation

Document your CSS code with comments. Comments provide context and explanations for your styles, making it easier for you and your team to understand and maintain the code.

```
/* Header styles */
.header {
    background-color: #3498db;
    /* ... */
}

/* Footer styles */
```

```
.footer {
    background-color: #333;
    /* ... */
}
```

3.6.6 Group Related Styles

Organize your styles by grouping related properties together.
For example, group all typography styles, padding and margin
properties, and background styles. This improves code
readability and helps you locate and update styles efficiently.

3.6.7 Responsive Design

When designing for different screen sizes, organize your media
queries logically. Consider using a mobile-first approach,
where you define styles for small screens initially and
progressively enhance them for larger screens.

```
/* Small screens */
.button {
    font-size: 16px;
    /* ... */
}

/* Medium screens */
@media screen and (min-width: 768px) {
    .button {
        font-size: 20px;
        /* ... */
    }
}
```

3.6.8 Version Control

Use a version control system like Git to track changes to your CSS files. This ensures that you can revert to previous versions if needed and collaborate effectively with others.

3.6.9 Minify and Optimize for Production

Before deploying your project to production, minify your CSS files to reduce file size and optimize page loading speed. Tools like UglifyCSS or online services can help with this task.

By following these best practices for CSS organization, you'll create maintainable, readable, and efficient stylesheets. Consistency and modularity are key, allowing you to scale your web development projects with ease and collaborate effectively with other team members. As you progress through this book, you'll continue to explore advanced CSS techniques and their integration with other web development technologies.

Chapter 4: JavaScript Fundamentals

4.1 Introduction to JavaScript

Welcome to the exciting world of JavaScript, the programming language that brings interactivity and dynamic functionality to your web development projects. In this section, we'll embark on a journey to explore the fundamental concepts of JavaScript and understand how it seamlessly integrates with HTML and CSS to create dynamic and engaging web experiences.

4.1.1 The Role of JavaScript

JavaScript is a versatile and powerful scripting language that runs directly in web browsers, making it an integral part of modern web development. It empowers you to:

- Enhance user interfaces with interactive elements like forms, buttons, and sliders.
- Retrieve and manipulate data from external sources or user inputs.
- Create animations, transitions, and real-time updates for a dynamic user experience.
- Implement client-side validation and error handling in web forms.
- Build single-page applications (SPAs) and web-based games.
- Communicate with web servers to fetch and send data asynchronously (AJAX).

4.1.2 JavaScript in the Web Development Stack

In the typical web development stack, JavaScript forms the "front end" or "client-side" part of the application. It runs directly in the user's web browser, complementing HTML (for structure) and CSS (for styling). Together, these three technologies create a seamless and interactive user experience.

4.1.3 Adding JavaScript to HTML

To include JavaScript in your HTML documents, you can use the <script> element. You can place JavaScript code within the HTML document's <head> or <body> section, or you can link to external JavaScript files.

```
<!DOCTYPE html>
<html>
<head>
    <title>My Web Page</title>
    <script>
        // JavaScript code goes here
        alert("Hello, World!");
    </script>
</head>
<body>
    <!-- HTML content -->
</body>
</html>
```

4.1.4 Basic JavaScript Syntax

JavaScript code consists of statements, which are instructions that the browser executes. Here's a simple example:

```
// This is a JavaScript comment
var message = "Hello, World!";
console.log(message); // Output the message to the
console
```

Key concepts in JavaScript include variables, data types, operators, control structures (if statements, loops), functions, and objects.

4.1.5 The Document Object Model (DOM)

One of JavaScript's most critical features is its ability to interact with the Document Object Model (DOM), which represents the structure of a web page. JavaScript can access and manipulate DOM elements, enabling you to dynamically update content and respond to user actions.

4.1.6 Asynchronous Programming

JavaScript is inherently asynchronous, meaning it can execute tasks simultaneously without blocking the main thread. This is crucial for tasks like handling user input, making network requests, and animating elements.

4.1.7 Browser Compatibility

JavaScript is supported by all modern web browsers. However, browser compatibility is essential, and you may need to use feature detection or polyfills to ensure consistent behavior across different browsers.

4.1.8 Resources and Further Learning

Throughout this book, we'll delve deeper into JavaScript's core concepts, best practices, and practical applications. You'll learn how to create interactive web applications, work with data, and leverage third-party libraries and frameworks to streamline your development process.

JavaScript is an essential skill for modern web developers, and as you dive into this chapter, you'll lay the foundation for creating dynamic and engaging web experiences. So, let's embark on this exciting journey into the world of JavaScript and unlock its limitless possibilities.

4.2 Variables, Data Types, and Operators

In the realm of JavaScript, variables, data types, and operators form the bedrock upon which you build your scripts. These fundamental elements enable you to store, manipulate, and process data dynamically. In this section, we'll delve into the core concepts of variables, data types, and operators in JavaScript.

4.2.1 Variables in JavaScript

Variables are like containers for storing data. They allow you to assign a name (identifier) to a value, making it easier to reference and manipulate that value in your code.

In JavaScript, you declare variables using the var, let, or const keyword, followed by a variable name. For example:

```
var age = 25; // Declare a variable 'age' and
assign it the value 25.
```

- var: Historically used for variable declaration but has some scoping issues.

- `let`: Introduced in ES6 (ECMAScript 2015) and provides block-level scoping.
- `const`: Also introduced in ES6 and used for constants whose values should not change.

4.2.2 Data Types

JavaScript has several data types, categorized as:

- **Primitive Data Types:**

  - **Numbers**: Representing numeric values (e.g., `3.14`, `42`).
  - **Strings**: Representing text (e.g., `"Hello, World!"`).
  - **Booleans**: Representing true or false values (`true`, `false`).
  - **Undefined**: A special value indicating that a variable has been declared but not assigned a value (`undefined`).
  - **Null**: A special value indicating the absence of any object value (`null`).
  - **Symbols**: Introduced in ES6, representing unique and immutable values.

- **Complex Data Types:**

  - **Objects**: Used to store collections of key-value pairs. Objects can contain other objects, arrays, functions, and more.

- **Arrays**: Special objects used to store ordered collections of values.

4.2.3 Operators

Operators are symbols that allow you to perform operations on variables and values. JavaScript supports a variety of operators, including:

- **Arithmetic Operators**: Used for basic mathematical calculations like addition, subtraction, multiplication, and division.

```
var x = 10;
var y = 5;
var sum = x + y; // Addition
var difference = x - y; // Subtraction
var product = x * y; // Multiplication
var quotient = x / y; // Division
```

- **Comparison Operators**: Used to compare values and return a Boolean result.

```
var a = 10;
var b = 5;
var isEqual = a === b; // Equality check
(false)
var isNotEqual = a !== b; // Inequality check
(true)
var isGreaterThan = a > b; // Greater than
(true)
var isLessThan = a < b; // Less than (false)
```

- **Logical Operators**: Used for combining and manipulating Boolean values.

```
var isTrue = true;
var isFalse = false;
var logicalAnd = isTrue && isFalse; //
Logical AND (false)
var logicalOr = isTrue || isFalse; // Logical
OR (true)
var logicalNot = !isTrue; // Logical NOT
(false)
```

- **Assignment Operators**: Used to assign values to variables.

```
var x = 10;
x += 5; // x is now 15 (same as x = x + 5)
```

- **Other Operators**: JavaScript also includes conditional (ternary) operators, bitwise operators, and more.

Understanding variables, data types, and operators is fundamental to working with JavaScript. These concepts provide the building blocks for creating dynamic scripts that manipulate data, make decisions, and respond to user interactions. As you progress through this chapter, you'll explore these fundamentals in more depth and discover how they can be applied to solve real-world programming challenges.

4.3 Control Structures: Conditionals and Loops

In the world of JavaScript, control structures empower you to dictate the flow of your code, make decisions, and execute repetitive tasks efficiently. This section explores two fundamental categories of control structures: conditionals and loops.

4.3.1 Conditional Statements

Conditional statements allow your JavaScript code to make decisions and execute different actions based on specified conditions. The most common conditional statement in JavaScript is the `if` statement.

- **if Statement:** The `if` statement checks a condition, and if it evaluates to `true`, it executes a block of code enclosed within curly braces.

```
var temperature = 25;

if (temperature > 30) {
    console.log("It's a hot day!");
} else if (temperature >= 20) {
    console.log("The weather is pleasant.");
} else {
    console.log("It's cold outside.");
}
```

- **Switch Statement:** The `switch` statement is used when you have multiple conditions to test against a single value.

```
var day = "Monday";

switch (day) {
    case "Monday":
        console.log("It's the start of the
week.");
        break;
    case "Friday":
        console.log("The weekend is almost
here.");
        break;
    default:
        console.log("It's a regular day.");
}
```

4.3.2 Loops

Loops are essential for executing a block of code repeatedly. JavaScript provides several loop types, but two of the most commonly used are `for` and `while` loops.

- **for Loop:** A `for` loop allows you to iterate over a range of values or elements.

```
for (var i = 1; i <= 5; i++) {
    console.log("Iteration #" + i);
}
```

- **while Loop:** A `while` loop continues to execute a block of code as long as a specified condition remains `true`.

```
var count = 0;

while (count < 5) {
    console.log("Count: " + count);
    count++;
}
```

- **do...while Loop:** Similar to a `while` loop, but it guarantees that the code block will execute at least once before checking the condition.

```
var number = 1;

do {
    console.log("Number: " + number);
    number++;
} while (number <= 3);
```

4.3.3 Control Flow and Nesting

You can combine conditionals and loops and nest them to create complex control flow structures. For example, you might use loops to iterate over an array and conditionals to perform actions based on each array element's value.

```
var numbers = [1, 2, 3, 4, 5];

for (var i = 0; i < numbers.length; i++) {
    if (numbers[i] % 2 === 0) {
        console.log(numbers[i] + " is even.");
    } else {
```

```
        console.log(numbers[i] + " is odd.");
    }
}
```

Control structures are essential for implementing dynamic, responsive, and interactive web applications. As you advance through this chapter, you'll explore more advanced control structures and learn how to use them effectively in real-world JavaScript programming scenarios.

4.4 Functions and Scope

Functions are the building blocks of JavaScript, allowing you to encapsulate reusable blocks of code. Understanding how functions work and how scope operates within JavaScript is crucial for writing clean, organized, and efficient code. In this section, we'll dive into the world of functions and scope.

4.4.1 Functions in JavaScript

A function is a block of code that can be called and executed when needed. Functions allow you to group statements together and reuse them, making your code more modular and maintainable. Here's how you define a simple function in JavaScript:

```
function greet(name) {
    console.log("Hello, " + name + "!");
}

// Calling the function
greet("Alice"); // Output: Hello, Alice!
```

- **Parameters:** Functions can accept parameters (also called arguments), which are placeholders for values you pass when calling the function. In the example above, `name` is a parameter.

- **Return Values:** Functions can also return values using the `return` statement. The returned value can be used elsewhere in your code.

```javascript
function add(a, b) {
    return a + b;
}

var result = add(3, 5);
console.log(result); // Output: 8
```

4.4.2 Function Scope

JavaScript uses function scope, meaning variables defined inside a function are only accessible within that function. This concept is often referred to as "local scope."

```javascript
function greet(name) {
    var message = "Hello, " + name + "!";
    console.log(message);
}

greet("Bob");
console.log(message); // Error: 'message' is not defined
```

In this example, `message` is only accessible within the `greet` function.

4.4.3 Global Scope

Variables declared outside of any function are said to have "global scope" and can be accessed from anywhere in your code.

```
var globalVar = "I'm global!";

function logGlobalVar() {
    console.log(globalVar);
}

logGlobalVar(); // Output: I'm global!
```

However, it's considered best practice to minimize the use of global variables to avoid potential conflicts and maintainability issues.

4.4.4 Function Expressions

In addition to defining functions with the `function` keyword, you can also create "function expressions." These are essentially functions assigned to variables.

```
var greet = function(name) {
    console.log("Hello, " + name + "!");
};

greet("Carol"); // Output: Hello, Carol!
```

Function expressions are useful for creating anonymous functions and passing them as arguments to other functions, like in event handling.

4.4.5 Closure

A closure is a fundamental concept in JavaScript. It occurs when a function "remembers" the variables in its outer scope even after the outer function has finished executing.

```
function outer() {
    var outerVar = "I'm from outer scope";

    function inner() {
        console.log(outerVar);
    }

    return inner;
}

var innerFunc = outer();
innerFunc(); // Output: I'm from outer scope
```

In this example, `inner` has access to `outerVar` even though `outer` has completed execution.

Understanding functions and scope is essential for effective JavaScript programming. Functions provide a way to structure and reuse code, while scope dictates where variables can be accessed. As you delve deeper into JavaScript, you'll encounter more advanced concepts related to functions, such as closures, callbacks, and promises, which play vital roles in creating sophisticated web applications.

4.5 Working with Arrays and Objects

Arrays and objects are fundamental data structures in JavaScript, allowing you to organize, manipulate, and store data efficiently. In this section, we'll explore how to work with arrays and objects, both of which are essential for building dynamic web applications.

4.5.1 Arrays

An array is an ordered list-like collection of values, each identified by an index. Arrays can hold various data types, including numbers, strings, objects, and even other arrays. Here's how you create and work with arrays:

- **Creating an Array:**

  ```
  var fruits = ["apple", "banana", "cherry"];
  ```

- **Accessing Elements:**

  ```
  var firstFruit = fruits[0]; // "apple"
  ```

- **Modifying Elements:**

  ```
  fruits[1] = "orange"; // Change "banana" to "orange"
  ```

- **Adding Elements:**

  ```
  fruits.push("grape"); // Add "grape" to the end
  ```

- **Iterating through an Array:**

  ```
  for (var i = 0; i < fruits.length; i++) {
      console.log(fruits[i]);
  }
  ```

- **Array Methods:** JavaScript provides a wealth of array methods for operations like sorting, filtering, mapping, and reducing.

4.5.2 Objects

An object is an unordered collection of key-value pairs, where each key is a unique identifier for a value. Objects are versatile and can represent various entities and their properties. Here's how you create and work with objects:

- **Creating an Object:**

```
var person = {
    firstName: "John",
    lastName: "Doe",
    age: 30,
};
```

- **Accessing Properties:**

```
var firstName = person.firstName; // "John"
```

- **Modifying Properties:**

```
person.age = 31; // Update the age property
```

- **Adding Properties:**

```
person.email = "john@example.com"; // Add an
email property
```

- **Iterating through Object Properties:** You can use loops or built-in methods like `Object.keys()` to iterate through an object's properties.

```
for (var key in person) {
    console.log(key + ": " + person[key]);
}
```

4.5.3 Combining Arrays and Objects

Arrays and objects are often used together to represent complex data structures. For example, you can create an array of objects to store a list of items, each with multiple properties.

```
var students = [
    { name: "Alice", age: 22 },
    { name: "Bob", age: 20 },
    { name: "Carol", age: 23 },
];
```

This array of objects represents a list of students with their respective names and ages.

Working effectively with arrays and objects is essential for managing data in your JavaScript applications. Whether you're building a shopping cart, a user management system, or any other dynamic feature, arrays and objects are your go-to tools for structuring and manipulating data. As you progress through this chapter, you'll discover advanced techniques for working with these data structures and using them to create dynamic web experiences.

4.6 Error Handling and Debugging

Error handling and debugging are crucial skills for any JavaScript developer. They allow you to identify, diagnose, and resolve issues in your code, ensuring your web applications function smoothly. In this section, we'll explore error handling strategies and debugging techniques to help you write robust and error-free JavaScript code.

4.6.1 Common Types of Errors

JavaScript errors can be categorized into three main types:

- **Syntax Errors:** These occur when your code violates the language's rules and structure. Syntax errors prevent the script from running at all and must be fixed before execution.

```
var x = 10;
console.log(x; // Syntax error: Missing
closing parenthesis
```

- **Runtime Errors:** Also known as exceptions, these errors occur during script execution when something unexpected happens, such as attempting to access a non-existent property of an object.

```
var data = { name: "Alice" };
console.log(data.age); // Runtime error:
'age' is undefined
```

- **Logical Errors:** These errors don't produce immediate error messages but cause the script to behave incorrectly. Identifying and fixing logical errors can be more challenging.

```
function calculateTotal(price, quantity) {
    return price * quantity;
}

var total = calculateTotal(10, "2"); //
Logical error: Incorrect result due to non-
numeric input
```

4.6.2 Error Handling

JavaScript provides a mechanism for handling runtime errors using `try...catch` blocks. With `try...catch`, you can "catch" exceptions and gracefully handle them to prevent the script from crashing.

```
try {
    // Code that might cause an error
    var result = x / y;
} catch (error) {
    // Handle the error
    console.error("An error occurred: " +
error.message);
}
```

- **throw Statement:** You can manually throw exceptions using the `throw` statement. This is useful when you want to create custom error messages or conditions.

```
function divide(x, y) {
    if (y === 0) {
```

```
        throw new Error("Division by zero is
not allowed.");
    }
    return x / y;
}
```

4.6.3 Debugging Techniques

Debugging is the process of identifying and fixing errors in your code. JavaScript offers several debugging techniques and tools:

- **Console Logging:** Use `console.log()` to print values and messages to the browser's console. This is a simple yet effective way to inspect variables and track the flow of your code.

  ```
  console.log("Starting the calculation...");
  var result = calculateTotal(10, 2);
  console.log("Result: " + result);
  ```

- **Breakpoints:** Most modern browsers include developer tools with features like breakpoints. You can set breakpoints in your code to pause execution and inspect variable values and call stacks.

- **Step Through Code:** Debugging tools allow you to step through your code one line at a time, making it easier to pinpoint issues.

- **Error Messages:** Pay attention to error messages in the console. They often provide valuable information about the type of error and its location.

- **Browser DevTools:** Browser developer tools offer comprehensive debugging features, including real-time inspection of DOM elements, network activity, and more.

- **Linters:** Utilize code analysis tools and linters like ESLint to catch common coding mistakes and enforce coding standards.

Debugging is a skill that improves with practice. As you encounter and resolve errors in your JavaScript code, you'll become more proficient at identifying issues and crafting efficient solutions. Error handling and debugging are essential aspects of JavaScript development that contribute to the reliability and performance of your web applications.

Chapter 5: DOM Manipulation with JavaScript

5.1 Document Object Model (DOM) Overview

In the realm of web development, the Document Object Model (DOM) plays a pivotal role in creating dynamic and interactive web applications. Understanding the DOM is essential for manipulating and controlling web page content using JavaScript. In this section, we'll provide an overview of the DOM, its structure, and its significance in web development.

5.1.1 What Is the DOM?

The Document Object Model (DOM) is a programming interface for web documents. It represents the structure of an HTML or XML document as a tree-like structure, with each part of the document represented as a node in the tree. These nodes can be elements, attributes, text content, and more.

5.1.2 DOM Tree Structure

The DOM tree structure consists of nodes organized hierarchically, with the following key node types:

- **Document Node:** The root of the DOM tree, representing the entire HTML document.
- **Element Nodes:** Represent HTML elements such as `<div>`, `<p>`, and `<h1>`. These nodes can have child nodes, including other elements or text nodes.
- **Text Nodes:** Contain text content within an element.
- **Attribute Nodes:** Represent attributes of an element, such as `id`, `class`, or `src`.

Here's a simplified representation of a DOM tree for a basic HTML document:

```
Document Node (HTML)
|
```

```
|-- Element Node (head)
|   |
|   |-- Element Node (title)
|   |   |
|   |   |-- Text Node ("Document Title")
|
|-- Element Node (body)
|   |
|   |-- Element Node (h1)
|   |   |
|   |   |-- Text Node ("Welcome to My Website")
|   |
|   |-- Element Node (p)
|   |   |
|   |   |-- Text Node ("This is a paragraph of
text.")
```

5.1.3 JavaScript and the DOM

JavaScript interacts with the DOM to manipulate the content and behavior of web pages. With JavaScript, you can:

- Access and modify HTML elements and attributes.
- Add or remove elements dynamically.
- Respond to user interactions, such as clicks and input events.
- Update the content of a web page in real time without requiring a page reload.

5.1.4 DOM Manipulation Example

Here's a simple example of how JavaScript can manipulate the DOM:

```
// Find an element by its ID
```

```
var heading = document.getElementById("main-
heading");

// Change its text content
heading.textContent = "New Heading Text";

// Add a CSS class
heading.classList.add("highlight");

// Create a new element
var paragraph = document.createElement("p");
paragraph.textContent = "This is a new paragraph.";

// Append it to the document
document.body.appendChild(paragraph);
```

In this example, JavaScript locates an HTML element by its ID, modifies its content and appearance, creates a new element, and appends it to the web page.

5.1.5 Browser Compatibility

The DOM is a standardized interface, but browser implementations can vary slightly. Modern web development practices often use libraries and frameworks to abstract these differences and provide a consistent API for working with the DOM across different browsers.

Understanding the DOM is fundamental for web development, as it enables you to create rich, interactive user interfaces. As you delve deeper into DOM manipulation with JavaScript, you'll learn more advanced techniques for creating dynamic web applications and responding to user interactions.

5.2 Selecting DOM Elements

Manipulating the Document Object Model (DOM) using JavaScript often begins with selecting specific DOM elements. These elements can be modified, updated, or manipulated in various ways. In this section, we'll explore different methods for selecting DOM elements with JavaScript.

5.2.1 getElementById

The `getElementById` method allows you to select an element based on its unique `id` attribute. This method returns a reference to the first element with the specified `id`.

```
// Select an element with the ID "my-element"
var element = document.getElementById("my-element");
```

5.2.2 getElementsByClassName

The `getElementsByClassName` method retrieves a collection of elements that share a specific class name. It returns an array-like object containing all matching elements.

```
// Select all elements with the class "highlight"
var elements = document.getElementsByClassName("highlight");
```

5.2.3 getElementsByTagName

The `getElementsByTagName` method returns a collection of elements with a particular HTML tag name, such as `<div>`, `<p>`, or `<a>`.

```
// Select all <p> elements in the document
var paragraphs =
document.getElementsByTagName("p");
```

5.2.4 querySelector

The `querySelector` method allows you to select the first element in the DOM that matches a specific CSS selector.

```
// Select the first <p> element with class "intro"
var introParagraph =
document.querySelector("p.intro");
```

5.2.5 querySelectorAll

Similar to `querySelector`, `querySelectorAll` selects all elements in the DOM that match a given CSS selector. It returns a collection of all matching elements.

```
// Select all elements with the class "btn"
var buttons = document.querySelectorAll(".btn");
```

5.2.6 Selecting Nested Elements

You can also select nested elements by chaining methods together. For example, to select a paragraph inside a specific <div> element:

```
// Select the first <p> element inside a <div> with
ID "content"
var paragraphInContent =
document.querySelector("#content p");
```

5.2.7 Selecting by Attribute

You can select elements based on their attributes using attribute selectors. For example, to select all <a> elements with the `target="_blank"` attribute:

```
// Select all <a> elements with target="_blank"
var linksWithTargetBlank =
document.querySelectorAll("a[target='_blank']");
```

5.2.8 Selecting by Parent-Child Relationships

You can traverse the DOM by selecting elements based on their parent-child relationships. For example, to select all direct child elements of a specific element:

```
// Select all direct child elements of an element
with ID "parent"
var children = document.querySelector("#parent >
*");
```

These are some of the methods available for selecting DOM elements with JavaScript. The choice of method depends on your specific needs and the structure of your HTML document. Once you've selected the elements you want to work with, you can manipulate their properties, content, and attributes, enabling you to create dynamic and interactive web applications.

5.3 Modifying and Manipulating DOM Elements

Once you've selected DOM elements using JavaScript, you can modify and manipulate them to create dynamic and interactive web applications. In this section, we'll explore how to make changes to DOM elements, update their content, attributes, and appearance.

5.3.1 Modifying Text Content

You can change the text content of an element using the `textContent` property. This property sets or retrieves the text between the opening and closing tags of an element.

```
// Select an element by ID
var element = document.getElementById("my-
element");

// Change its text content
element.textContent = "New Text Content";
```

5.3.2 Modifying HTML Content

To change the HTML content of an element, use the `innerHTML` property. This property allows you to set or retrieve the HTML content within an element.

```
// Select an element by class name
var element = document.getElementsByClassName("my-
class")[0];

// Change its HTML content
element.innerHTML = "<p>New HTML Content</p>";
```

5.3.3 Modifying Attributes

You can change element attributes using the `setAttribute` method or by directly modifying the attribute properties.

```
// Select an element by tag name
var link = document.getElementsByTagName("a")[0];

// Using setAttribute
link.setAttribute("href",
"https://www.example.com");

// Using the attribute property
link.href = "https://www.example.com";
```

5.3.4 Modifying CSS Styles

You can dynamically change the CSS styles of elements by manipulating their `style` property.

```
// Select an element by ID
var element = document.getElementById("my-
element");

// Change its background color
element.style.backgroundColor = "blue";

// Change its font size
element.style.fontSize = "16px";
```

5.3.5 Adding and Removing Classes

To add or remove CSS classes from an element, use the `classList` property, which provides methods like `add()` and `remove()`.

```
// Select an element by class name
```

115

```
var element = document.getElementsByClassName("my-
class")[0];

// Add a class
element.classList.add("new-class");

// Remove a class
element.classList.remove("old-class");
```

5.3.6 Creating and Appending Elements

You can create new elements using the createElement
method and add them to the DOM using methods like
appendChild.

```
// Create a new paragraph element
var paragraph = document.createElement("p");
paragraph.textContent = "New Paragraph";

// Append it to an existing element
var container =
document.getElementById("container");
container.appendChild(paragraph);
```

5.3.7 Removing Elements

To remove elements from the DOM, you can use the
remove() method.

```
// Select an element to remove
var elementToRemove =
document.getElementById("element-to-remove");

// Remove it from the DOM
elementToRemove.remove();
```

These are fundamental techniques for modifying and manipulating DOM elements with JavaScript. By combining these methods, you can create interactive web applications that respond to user actions, update content dynamically, and provide a seamless user experience.

5.4 Event Handling

In web development, event handling is a fundamental concept that allows you to create interactive and dynamic web applications. Events are user actions or occurrences on a web page, such as clicks, mouse movements, keyboard input, or page loading. In this section, we'll explore how to handle events in JavaScript to make your web applications responsive to user interactions.

5.4.1 Understanding Events

Events are triggered by various actions on a web page and can be associated with specific HTML elements. Some common events include:

- **Click:** Triggered when the mouse button is clicked on an element.
- **Mouseover:** Fired when the mouse pointer enters an element.
- **Mouseout:** Fired when the mouse pointer leaves an element.
- **Keydown/Keyup:** Raised when a keyboard key is pressed/released.

- **Submit:** Triggered when a form is submitted.
- **Load:** Fired when a web page or an image finishes loading.

5.4.2 Event Handling in JavaScript

To respond to events, you attach event handlers or listeners to specific elements in your HTML document. Event handlers are JavaScript functions that execute when a particular event occurs. Here's how you can add an event listener to an element:

```javascript
// Select an element by ID
var button = document.getElementById("my-button");

// Add a click event listener
button.addEventListener("click", function() {
    alert("Button clicked!");
});
```

In this example, when the button with the ID "my-button" is clicked, the associated function is executed.

5.4.3 Event Object

When an event occurs, an event object is automatically created and passed to the event handler as a parameter. This object contains information about the event, such as the type of event, target element, and additional data.

```javascript
document.addEventListener("keydown",
function(event) {
    console.log("Key pressed: " + event.key);
});
```

In this code, the event object provides information about which key was pressed.

5.4.4 Event Propagation

Events in the DOM propagate through a hierarchy of elements, starting from the target element (where the event occurs) and moving up the tree to the root of the document. This process is known as event propagation and involves two phases: capturing and bubbling.

- **Capturing Phase:** Events are captured from the root to the target element.
- **Bubbling Phase:** Events bubble up from the target element to the root.

You can specify whether you want to listen for events during the capturing phase, the bubbling phase, or both when adding an event listener.

```
// Add a click event listener during the capturing
phase
element.addEventListener("click", myFunction,
true);

// Add a click event listener during the bubbling
phase
element.addEventListener("click", myFunction,
false);
```

5.4.5 Event Delegation

Event delegation is a technique where you attach a single event listener to a common ancestor of multiple elements rather than

119

attaching listeners to each individual element. This is particularly useful when you have dynamically created a large number of elements to which you want to apply the same event handler.

```
// Event delegation example
var container =
document.getElementById("container");

container.addEventListener("click", function(event)
{
    if (event.target.tagName === "BUTTON") {
        alert("Button clicked!");
    }
});
```

In this example, clicks on any button inside the container are handled by a single event listener attached to the container element.

5.4.6 Preventing Default Behavior

In some cases, you may want to prevent the default behavior of an event, such as preventing a form from submitting or a link from navigating to a new page. You can achieve this by calling event.preventDefault() within your event handler.

```
// Prevent a form from submitting
document.getElementById("my-
form").addEventListener("submit", function(event) {
    event.preventDefault();
    // Additional code to handle form submission
});
```

Event handling is a crucial aspect of web development, enabling you to create responsive and interactive user interfaces. By understanding how to handle events, you can build web applications that respond to user actions, provide real-time feedback, and enhance the overall user experience.

5.5 Asynchronous JavaScript and AJAX

Asynchronous JavaScript and AJAX (Asynchronous JavaScript and XML) are essential concepts in modern web development that allow you to retrieve and manipulate data from web servers without requiring a full page reload. In this section, we'll explore how to work with asynchronous JavaScript and make AJAX requests to create dynamic web applications.

5.5.1 Asynchronous JavaScript

JavaScript is single-threaded, which means it executes one task at a time in a sequential manner. However, certain operations, such as network requests and file loading, can be time-consuming. To avoid blocking the main thread and freezing the user interface, JavaScript employs asynchronous programming techniques.

5.5.2 Callback Functions

One common approach to asynchronous programming is using callback functions. Callbacks are functions that are passed as arguments to other functions and are executed when a specific task is completed.

```
// Example of a callback function
```

```
function fetchData(callback) {
    // Simulate a network request
    setTimeout(function() {
        var data = { name: "Alice", age: 30 };
        callback(data);
    }, 1000);
}

// Usage of the callback
fetchData(function(data) {
    console.log("Data received:", data);
});
```

In this example, `fetchData` simulates a network request and calls the provided callback function when the data is available.

5.5.3 Promises

Promises provide a more structured way to handle asynchronous operations and avoid callback hell (nested callbacks). A promise represents a future value or error and provides methods for handling the result or failure.

```
// Example using Promises
function fetchData() {
    return new Promise(function(resolve, reject) {
        // Simulate a network request
        setTimeout(function() {
            var data = { name: "Bob", age: 25 };
            resolve(data);
        }, 1000);
    });
}

// Usage of Promises
fetchData()
    .then(function(data) {
```

```
            console.log("Data received:", data);
        })
        .catch(function(error) {
            console.error("Error:", error);
        });
```

5.5.4 AJAX (Asynchronous JavaScript and XML)

AJAX is a technique for making asynchronous requests to a web server from within a web page. It enables you to fetch data and update parts of a web page without reloading the entire page. While the name suggests XML, modern AJAX requests often use JSON for data interchange due to its simplicity and efficiency.

```
// Example of an AJAX request using the Fetch API
(modern approach)
fetch("https://api.example.com/data")
    .then(function(response) {
        if (!response.ok) {
            throw new Error("Network response was
not ok");
        }
        return response.json();
    })
    .then(function(data) {
        console.log("Data received:", data);
    })
    .catch(function(error) {
        console.error("Error:", error);
    });
```

In this example, the Fetch API is used to make an AJAX request to retrieve data from a remote server and handle the response asynchronously.

5.5.5 Updating the DOM with AJAX

Once you've fetched data via AJAX, you can use JavaScript to update the DOM with the new information, creating dynamic and responsive web applications.

```
fetch("https://api.example.com/news")
    .then(function(response) {
        if (!response.ok) {
            throw new Error("Network response was
not ok");
        }
        return response.json();
    })
    .then(function(newsData) {
        // Update the DOM with the fetched newsData
        var newsList =
document.getElementById("news-list");
        newsData.forEach(function(newsItem) {
            var listItem =
document.createElement("li");
            listItem.textContent = newsItem.title;
            newsList.appendChild(listItem);
        });
    })
    .catch(function(error) {
        console.error("Error:", error);
    });
```

This example demonstrates how to fetch news data from a server and update an HTML list (<ul>) with the retrieved news titles.

Asynchronous JavaScript and AJAX are powerful tools that allow you to create web applications that can fetch and update data without interrupting the user experience. Understanding these concepts is essential for building responsive and dynamic web applications that interact with remote servers and provide real-time updates to users.

5.6 DOM Traversal and Manipulation Techniques

DOM traversal and manipulation are essential skills for web developers. These techniques allow you to navigate the Document Object Model (DOM) and make dynamic changes to web pages. In this section, we'll explore various methods and approaches for traversing and manipulating the DOM using JavaScript.

5.6.1 Traversing the DOM

DOM traversal involves moving through the DOM tree to access specific elements or their relationships. Here are some common methods for traversing the DOM:

- **parentNode and childNodes:** These properties allow you to navigate up and down the DOM tree to access parent and child elements.

  ```
  var parent = document.getElementById("parent-element");
  var children = parent.childNodes; // Returns a NodeList of child nodes
  ```

- **querySelector and querySelectorAll:** These methods enable you to select elements using CSS-style selectors.

```
var element = document.querySelector(".my-
class"); // Selects the first element with
class "my-class"
var elements =
document.querySelectorAll("p"); // Selects
all <p> elements
```

- **nextSibling and previousSibling:** These properties provide access to adjacent sibling elements.

```
var currentElement =
document.getElementById("current-element");
var nextElement = currentElement.nextSibling;
// Access the next sibling
var prevElement =
currentElement.previousSibling; // Access the
previous sibling
```

- **parentElement:** This property allows you to directly access the parent element of a node.

```
var child = document.getElementById("child-
element");
var parent = child.parentElement; // Access
the parent element
```

- **Traversing up the DOM:** You can traverse up the DOM tree using a loop, starting from a specific element and moving toward the root.

```
var current = document.getElementById("child-
element");
```

```
while (current.parentNode) {
    console.log(current.nodeName);
    current = current.parentNode;
}
```

5.6.2 Modifying the DOM

Once you've traversed to the desired element, you can manipulate it in various ways. Here are some common methods for modifying the DOM:

- **createElement:** Create a new HTML element.

  ```
  var newDiv = document.createElement("div");
  ```

- **appendChild and removeChild:** Add or remove child elements from a parent element.

  ```
  var parent = document.getElementById("parent-
  element");
  var child = document.getElementById("child-
  element");

  parent.appendChild(child); // Add child to
  parent
  parent.removeChild(child); // Remove child
  from parent
  ```

- **setAttribute and removeAttribute:** Modify or remove attributes of an element.

  ```
  var link = document.getElementById("my-
  link");
  link.setAttribute("href",
  "https://www.example.com");
  ```

127

```
link.removeAttribute("target");
```

- **classList:** Manipulate CSS classes of elements.

```
var element = document.getElementById("my-
element");
element.classList.add("new-class");
element.classList.remove("old-class");
```

- **textContent and innerHTML:** Change the text content or HTML content of an element.

```
var paragraph = document.getElementById("my-
paragraph");
paragraph.textContent = "New text content";
paragraph.innerHTML = "<strong>New HTML
content</strong>";
```

- **style:** Modify inline CSS styles of elements.

```
var element = document.getElementById("my-
element");
element.style.color = "red";
element.style.backgroundColor = "yellow";
```

DOM traversal and manipulation techniques are essential for creating dynamic and interactive web pages. Whether you need to select specific elements, modify their content, or change their appearance, a solid understanding of these techniques will empower you to build engaging web applications that respond to user interactions and data changes.

Chapter 6: Interactive Web Development

Interactive web development is a pivotal aspect of modern web development, focusing on creating dynamic and engaging web experiences for users. In this chapter, we delve into the world of interactivity, exploring the technologies and techniques that enable developers to build interactive web applications using HTML, CSS, and JavaScript.

129

6.1 Form Validation with JavaScript

Form validation is a critical aspect of web development, ensuring that user-submitted data meets specific criteria or constraints before it's sent to the server. JavaScript plays a vital role in enhancing the user experience by providing real-time feedback and preventing invalid data submission. In this section, we'll explore how to perform form validation using JavaScript.

6.1.1 Why Form Validation?

Form validation serves several essential purposes:

- **Data Integrity:** It ensures that the data submitted by users adheres to the expected format and constraints, preventing incorrect or malicious data from reaching the server.

- **User Experience:** Real-time validation provides immediate feedback to users, reducing the chances of errors and improving the overall user experience.

- **Reducing Server Load:** By catching errors on the client side, you reduce unnecessary server requests, improving efficiency and saving resources.

6.1.2 Basic Validation Techniques

Here are some common techniques for performing form validation with JavaScript:

- **Required Fields:** Check if required fields are filled in by verifying that they are not empty.

```
var nameField =
document.getElementById("name");

if (nameField.value === "") {
    alert("Name is required.");
    return false; // Prevent form submission
}
```

- **Email Validation:** Ensure that email addresses are in a valid format using regular expressions.

```
var emailField =
document.getElementById("email");
var emailPattern = /^[a-zA-Z0-9._-]+@[a-zA-Z0-9.-]+\.[a-zA-Z]{2,4}$/;

if (!emailPattern.test(emailField.value)) {
    alert("Invalid email address.");
    return false; // Prevent form submission
}
```

- **Password Strength:** Enforce strong password policies, such as minimum length and character requirements.

```
var passwordField =
document.getElementById("password");

if (passwordField.value.length < 8) {
    alert("Password must be at least 8
characters long.");
    return false; // Prevent form submission
}
```

6.1.3 Real-time Validation

Real-time validation provides immediate feedback to users as they interact with the form. You can achieve this by adding event listeners to form fields and validating data as it's entered or modified.

```
var emailField = document.getElementById("email");

emailField.addEventListener("input", function() {
    var emailPattern = /^[a-zA-Z0-9._-]+@[a-zA-Z0-
9.-]+\.[a-zA-Z]{2,4}$/;
    if (!emailPattern.test(emailField.value)) {
        emailField.setCustomValidity("Invalid email
address.");
    } else {
        emailField.setCustomValidity(""); // Clear
custom validation message
    }
});
```

In this example, as the user types into the email field, the script validates the input and displays a custom error message if the email format is invalid.

6.1.4 Displaying Error Messages

You can display error messages next to the problematic form fields to provide clear feedback to users.

```
<div>
    <label for="email">Email:</label>
    <input type="email" id="email" name="email"
required>
    <span class="error-message" id="email-
error"></span>
</div>
```

```
var emailField = document.getElementById("email");
var emailError = document.getElementById("email-
error");

emailField.addEventListener("input", function() {
    var emailPattern = /^[a-zA-Z0-9._-]+@[a-zA-Z0-
9.-]+\.[a-zA-Z]{2,4}$/;
    if (!emailPattern.test(emailField.value)) {
        emailError.textContent = "Invalid email
address.";
    } else {
        emailError.textContent = "";
    }
});
```

6.1.5 Submission Handling

After performing client-side validation, you can decide whether
to allow the form submission to proceed or prevent it based on
the validation results. You can return t rue to allow
submission or false to prevent it.

```
var form = document.getElementById("my-form");

form.addEventListener("submit", function(event) {
    // Perform validation checks
    if (/* validation fails */) {
        event.preventDefault(); // Prevent form
submission
    }
});
```

Form validation with JavaScript enhances the user experience
by providing immediate feedback and ensuring data integrity.
By implementing validation rules and techniques, you can

create web forms that are more user-friendly and robust, reducing the likelihood of errors and invalid submissions.

6.2 Creating Dynamic Content

Creating dynamic content is a core aspect of modern web development that allows you to build interactive and engaging web applications. Dynamic content refers to elements on a web page that can change or update without requiring a full page reload. JavaScript is a key tool for achieving dynamic content, and in this section, we'll explore various techniques for creating it.

6.2.1 Why Dynamic Content?

Dynamic content is essential for improving user engagement and interactivity. It allows you to:

- **Update Data:** Display real-time data, such as news feeds, social media updates, or stock prices.

- **Enhance User Experience:** Provide dynamic features like autocomplete, live search results, and interactive forms.

- **Build Single-Page Applications (SPAs):** Create web applications that load and update content seamlessly without page transitions.

6.2.2 Techniques for Creating Dynamic Content

Here are some techniques for creating dynamic content using JavaScript:

6.2.2.1 DOM Manipulation:

- **Updating Text and HTML:** You can use JavaScript to change the text or HTML content of an element dynamically. For example, you can update the text of a heading, paragraph, or a div.

```
var dynamicText = "Hello, Dynamic World!";
document.getElementById("my-
element").textContent = dynamicText;
```

- **Creating and Appending Elements:** JavaScript allows you to create new elements and append them to the DOM. This is useful for adding elements like lists, images, or even entire sections dynamically.

```
var newParagraph =
document.createElement("p");
newParagraph.textContent = "This is a new
paragraph.";
document.getElementById("content").appendChil
d(newParagraph);
```

6.2.2.2 Event Handling:

- **Responding to User Interactions:** Dynamic content often involves responding to user interactions, such as clicks, mouse movements, or form submissions. You can attach event listeners to elements to trigger actions in response to these events.

```
document.getElementById("my-
button").addEventListener("click", function()
{
    // Perform an action when the button is
clicked
    alert("Button clicked!");
});
```

6.2.2.3 AJAX and Fetch API:

- **Fetching Data:** To display real-time data from a server without a page refresh, you can use AJAX or the modern Fetch API to retrieve data from an API endpoint and then update the DOM with the received data.

```
fetch("https://api.example.com/news")
    .then(function(response) {
        return response.json();
    })
    .then(function(newsData) {
        // Update the DOM with the received
newsData
        var newsList =
document.getElementById("news-list");
        newsData.forEach(function(newsItem) {
            var listItem =
document.createElement("li");
            listItem.textContent =
newsItem.title;
            newsList.appendChild(listItem);
        });
    })
    .catch(function(error) {
```

```
        console.error("Error:", error);
    });
```

6.2.2.4 Templates and Frameworks:

- **Using Templates:** Many JavaScript frameworks and libraries, such as React, Angular, and Vue.js, offer templating solutions that make it easier to create dynamic content. These frameworks allow you to define templates for components and render them based on data.

```
// Example using React
const element = <p>Hello, Dynamic World!</p>;
ReactDOM.render(element,
document.getElementById("root"));
```

6.2.3 Benefits of Dynamic Content

Creating dynamic content using JavaScript provides several benefits:

- **Improved User Experience:** Users see updated information without page reloads, making interactions more seamless.

- **Real-time Updates:** Display real-time data, like live chat messages or stock prices.

- **Interactive Forms:** Enhance forms with real-time validation, autocomplete, and error messages.

- **Reduced Server Load:** Fetch only the data needed, reducing the load on the server and improving performance.

Dynamic content is a fundamental aspect of modern web development. It empowers you to create web applications that respond to user actions, provide real-time updates, and offer a more interactive and engaging user experience.

6.3 Working with Cookies and Local Storage

Cookies and local storage are client-side storage mechanisms in web development that allow you to store and manage data on the user's device. In this section, we'll explore how to work with cookies and local storage using JavaScript to enhance user experiences and persist data between sessions.

6.3.1 Cookies

Cookies are small pieces of data that websites store on a user's device. They are sent with each HTTP request, allowing you to store information on the client side. Here's how you can work with cookies in JavaScript:

- **Setting Cookies:**

  You can set cookies using the `document.cookie` property. Cookies are typically stored as key-value pairs, and you can include additional information like expiration date and domain.

```
document.cookie = "username=John;
expires=Thu, 01 Jan 2025 00:00:00 UTC;
path=/";
```

- **Reading Cookies:**

  To read cookies, you can access the
  document.cookie property, which contains all the
  cookies for the current domain.

  ```
  var allCookies = document.cookie;
  ```

- **Deleting Cookies:**

  To delete a cookie, you can set its expiration date to a
  past date.

  ```
  document.cookie = "username=; expires=Thu, 01
  Jan 1970 00:00:00 UTC; path=/;";
  ```

Cookies are widely used for tasks like session management,
remembering user preferences, and tracking user behavior.

6.3.2 Local Storage

Local storage is a more modern and flexible way to store data
on the client side. Unlike cookies, local storage has a larger
capacity and is not sent with every HTTP request. Here's how
you can work with local storage in JavaScript:

- **Setting and Retrieving Data:**

Local storage stores data as key-value pairs, and you can use the `localStorage` object to set and retrieve data.

```
// Set data
localStorage.setItem("username", "John");

// Retrieve data
var username =
localStorage.getItem("username");
```

- **Removing Data:**

  You can remove data from local storage using the `removeItem()` method or clear all data for a specific domain using `clear()`.

```
// Remove a specific item
localStorage.removeItem("username");

// Clear all data for the current domain
localStorage.clear();
```

- **Limitations:**

  While local storage is a powerful tool for storing client-side data, it has some limitations. Data is stored as strings, so you'll need to serialize and parse complex objects. Additionally, data in local storage is not shared between different tabs or windows of the same browser.

6.3.3 Use Cases

Here are some common use cases for cookies and local storage:

- **Cookies:**

  - Remembering user login sessions.
  - Storing user preferences, such as theme or language settings.
  - Tracking user behavior for analytics and advertising.

- **Local Storage:**

  - Caching data to improve app performance.
  - Storing user-generated content before submission.
  - Implementing a shopping cart in an e-commerce application.

6.3.4 Security Considerations

When working with cookies and local storage, it's essential to consider security:

- **Sensitive Data:** Avoid storing sensitive information like passwords or personal identification in cookies or local storage.

- **Secure and HttpOnly Cookies:** Use the Secure and HttpOnly flags for cookies when applicable to enhance security.

- **Data Validation:** Always validate and sanitize data before storing or using it to prevent security vulnerabilities.

Cookies and local storage are valuable tools for enhancing user experiences and persisting data on the client side. By understanding when and how to use them, you can build web applications that remember user preferences, provide seamless experiences, and improve overall user satisfaction.

6.4 Introduction to APIs

Application Programming Interfaces (APIs) are a fundamental component of modern web development, enabling communication between different software systems and allowing web applications to access external data and services. In this section, we'll introduce the concept of APIs and how they play a crucial role in building interactive web applications.

6.4.1 What is an API?

An API, short for Application Programming Interface, is a set of rules and protocols that allows one software application to interact with another. It defines the methods and data formats that applications can use to request and exchange information. APIs serve as intermediaries that enable different software systems to work together seamlessly.

6.4.2 Why Use APIs?

APIs are essential for several reasons:

- **Data Access:** APIs provide access to data and services that may not be available locally or within the application itself. This allows developers to incorporate external data into their applications.

- **Integration:** APIs enable the integration of various software systems, allowing them to share and exchange information efficiently.

- **Reuse:** Instead of reinventing the wheel, developers can leverage existing APIs to add features and functionalities to their applications without starting from scratch.

- **Scalability:** APIs make it possible to scale applications by connecting to external resources or services that can handle increased demand.

6.4.3 Types of APIs

There are various types of APIs, including:

- **Web APIs:** These are APIs that are accessible over the internet and are typically used to retrieve data from remote servers. Examples include social media APIs (e.g., Twitter API, Facebook Graph API) and data APIs (e.g., weather APIs, financial market data APIs).

- **Library APIs:** These APIs provide access to libraries or frameworks that developers can use within their applications. For instance, JavaScript libraries like jQuery have APIs for DOM manipulation and AJAX requests.

- **Operating System APIs:** These APIs allow applications to interact with the underlying operating system to perform tasks such as file access, hardware control, and network communication.

- **Hardware APIs:** Hardware APIs enable communication with hardware components like cameras, GPS devices, and sensors on mobile devices.

6.4.4 Working with Web APIs

Web APIs are particularly prevalent in web development. To work with a web API, developers typically follow these steps:

- **Authentication:** Many APIs require authentication to access their data or services. This can involve obtaining API keys, tokens, or other credentials.

- **Sending Requests:** Developers use HTTP requests (typically GET, POST, PUT, or DELETE) to communicate with the API. They specify the endpoint URL, parameters, and request headers.

- **Handling Responses:** APIs return responses in a specific format, often JSON or XML. Developers parse these responses to extract the data they need.

- **Error Handling:** It's essential to handle errors gracefully and provide feedback to users when API requests fail.

6.4.5 Use Cases for APIs

APIs are used in various scenarios, such as:

- **Social Media Integration:** Integrating social media platforms like Twitter or Facebook into web applications.

- **Payment Processing:** Implementing payment gateways like PayPal or Stripe.

- **Maps and Location Services:** Utilizing APIs like Google Maps for location-based features.

- **Data Retrieval:** Accessing external data sources, such as weather forecasts, stock market data, or news feeds.

- **Authentication:** Implementing third-party authentication providers like OAuth or OpenID Connect.

Understanding APIs and how to work with them is essential for web developers, as they open up a world of possibilities for creating dynamic and feature-rich web applications that can access external data and services, providing richer user experiences.

6.5 Building Interactive Web Applications

Building interactive web applications is the culmination of various web development skills, including HTML, CSS,

JavaScript, and API integration. In this section, we'll explore the process of building interactive web applications and discuss key concepts and best practices.

6.5.1 Interactive Web Applications: An Overview

Interactive web applications are dynamic and responsive web solutions that engage users, provide real-time feedback, and offer seamless experiences. These applications often incorporate features such as:

- **User Interactivity:** Users can perform actions, input data, and receive immediate feedback.

- **Data Presentation:** Data is presented dynamically, and updates occur without page reloads.

- **Third-Party Integrations:** External data sources or services are integrated through APIs.

- **User Authentication and Authorization:** Users can register, log in, and access personalized content.

6.5.2 Key Components of Interactive Web Applications

To build interactive web applications, you'll need to work with several key components:

- **HTML:** Structure your web page content using HTML to define the layout and elements.

- **CSS:** Apply styles and layouts to your HTML elements using CSS for a visually appealing and responsive design.

- **JavaScript:** Add interactivity and dynamic behavior to your web page using JavaScript. This includes event handling, DOM manipulation, and API integration.

- **APIs:** Integrate external data and services into your application using APIs. This can include web APIs for data retrieval and third-party services like authentication providers.

- **Server-Side Code:** If your application requires server-side processing, you'll need to implement server-side code, such as using Node.js, Python, Ruby, or PHP, to handle requests and manage data.

6.5.3 Building Blocks of Interactive Features

Interactive web applications often rely on the following building blocks:

- **Event Handling:** Use JavaScript to capture user actions like clicks, key presses, or form submissions and respond with the desired behavior.

- **Form Validation:** Implement client-side form validation to provide immediate feedback to users and prevent invalid submissions.

- **Dynamic Content:** Update content without page reloads by manipulating the DOM, fetching and displaying data from APIs, and utilizing client-side templates.

- **User Authentication:** Allow users to register, log in, and access personalized content while ensuring security and privacy.

- **Real-Time Updates:** Use technologies like WebSockets to enable real-time communication between clients and servers for features like chat or live notifications.

- **Optimization:** Optimize your application for performance, ensuring fast load times and efficient use of resources.

6.5.4 Best Practices for Interactive Web Development

When building interactive web applications, consider the following best practices:

- **Responsive Design:** Ensure your application works well on various devices and screen sizes by implementing responsive design principles.

- **Accessibility:** Make your application accessible to all users, including those with disabilities, by following web accessibility guidelines.

- **Security:** Implement security best practices to protect against common web vulnerabilities like cross-site scripting (XSS) and cross-site request forgery (CSRF).

- **Testing:** Thoroughly test your application, including functionality, compatibility, and performance, using testing frameworks and tools.

- **Scalability:** Design your application with scalability in mind to handle increased traffic and data.

- **Documentation:** Provide clear documentation for developers, including API documentation if applicable.

- **User Feedback:** Collect and incorporate user feedback to continuously improve your application.

6.5.5 Tools and Frameworks

There are various tools and frameworks available to simplify the development of interactive web applications, such as React, Angular, Vue.js, and libraries like jQuery and Bootstrap. These tools can streamline development and help you create rich user interfaces and experiences.

Building interactive web applications is an exciting and rewarding endeavor in web development. By mastering the core technologies, best practices, and tools, you can create web applications that engage users, deliver real-time information, and provide seamless and enjoyable experiences.

Chapter 7: Front-End Frameworks and Libraries

Front-end frameworks and libraries are essential tools in modern web development. In this chapter, we'll explore the role and significance of these tools in building dynamic and responsive web applications using HTML, CSS, and JavaScript.

7.1 Introduction to Front-End Frameworks (e.g., React, Vue, Angular)

Front-end development has evolved significantly over the years, with the emergence of powerful frameworks and libraries that have revolutionized how web applications are built. In this section, we will explore the role and importance of front-end frameworks, including some prominent examples like React, Vue, and Angular, in modern web development.

7.1.1 The Changing Landscape of Front-End Development

Front-end development, traditionally centered around HTML, CSS, and JavaScript, has become increasingly complex due to the demands of creating highly interactive and responsive web applications. As web applications have grown in complexity, developers have sought tools and methodologies to streamline the development process.

7.1.2 What Are Front-End Frameworks?

Front-end frameworks are comprehensive collections of pre-written code, templates, and guidelines that simplify and standardize the development of web user interfaces. They provide a structured approach to building web applications and promote best practices in areas such as architecture, code organization, and scalability.

7.1.3 Key Front-End Frameworks

Several front-end frameworks have gained prominence in recent years. Here are three notable examples:

- **React:** Developed by Facebook, React is a JavaScript library for building user interfaces. It allows developers to create reusable UI components and efficiently update the DOM, making it ideal for building single-page applications (SPAs) and dynamic web experiences.

- **Vue:** Vue.js is a progressive JavaScript framework that focuses on the view layer of an application. It is known for its simplicity and approachability, making it an excellent choice for both small projects and large-scale applications. Vue's component-based architecture encourages code reusability and maintainability.

- **Angular:** Angular, developed and maintained by Google, is a comprehensive front-end framework for building robust web applications. It offers a complete solution for building complex SPAs, including powerful features for data binding, dependency injection, and routing.

7.1.4 Why Use Front-End Frameworks?

Front-end frameworks offer several compelling advantages:

- **Efficiency:** Frameworks provide reusable components and a clear structure, reducing development time and effort.

- **Maintainability:** They enforce best practices, making code easier to maintain and scale as the application grows.

- **Performance:** Many frameworks optimize rendering and minimize unnecessary DOM updates, leading to faster and more efficient web applications.

- **Community Support:** Popular frameworks have active communities, providing access to extensive documentation, tutorials, and a wealth of resources.

7.1.5 Choosing the Right Framework

Selecting the right front-end framework depends on several factors, including project requirements, team expertise, and development goals. It's essential to evaluate each framework's strengths and weaknesses and consider how well it aligns with the specific needs of your project.

Front-end frameworks have transformed the landscape of web development, enabling developers to build sophisticated and responsive web applications more efficiently than ever before. In this chapter, we will dive deeper into these frameworks, exploring their core concepts, features, and practical use cases, to equip you with the knowledge and skills needed to leverage them effectively in your web development projects.

7.2 Using jQuery for DOM Manipulation

While modern front-end frameworks like React, Vue, and Angular have gained prominence, jQuery remains a valuable tool for simplifying DOM manipulation and enhancing interactivity in web development. In this section, we'll explore how to use jQuery effectively for DOM manipulation and its role in modern web development.

7.2.1 Introduction to jQuery

jQuery is a fast and concise JavaScript library that simplifies DOM traversal, manipulation, and event handling. It was created to address cross-browser compatibility issues and streamline common tasks that web developers face when working with the DOM.

7.2.2 Key Features of jQuery

jQuery offers a range of features that make it a popular choice for DOM manipulation:

- **DOM Traversal:** jQuery provides a set of methods for easily navigating and selecting elements within the DOM, such as `$(element)`, `parent()`, `children()`, and `find()`.

- **DOM Manipulation:** You can manipulate DOM elements with jQuery using methods like `html()`, `text()`, `addClass()`, `removeClass()`, `attr()`, and `css()`.

- **Event Handling:** jQuery simplifies event handling with methods like `click()`, `hover()`, `on()`, and `off()`, making it easier to respond to user interactions.

- **AJAX Requests:** jQuery includes AJAX utilities for making asynchronous requests to the server, enabling real-time updates without page refreshes.

- **Animation:** jQuery provides animation methods like `fadeIn()`, `fadeOut()`, `slideUp()`, and `slideDown()` for creating smooth transitions and effects.

7.2.3 Benefits of Using jQuery

jQuery offers several benefits for web developers:

- **Cross-Browser Compatibility:** jQuery abstracts many browser-specific quirks, ensuring that your code works consistently across different browsers.

- **Productivity:** It simplifies common tasks, reducing the amount of code you need to write and speeding up development.

- **Community and Plugins:** jQuery has a vast community and a rich ecosystem of plugins, extending its functionality for various use cases.

- **Legacy Code:** For projects that still rely on jQuery or have extensive legacy code, jQuery remains a practical choice.

7.2.4 Using jQuery for DOM Manipulation

Here's a brief overview of how jQuery can be used for DOM manipulation:

- **Selecting Elements:**

```
// Selecting an element by its ID
$("#elementId");

// Selecting elements by class
$(".className");

// Selecting elements by tag name
$("tagName");
```

- **Modifying Elements:**

```
// Changing text content
$("#elementId").text("New text");

// Adding or removing classes
$("#elementId").addClass("newClass");
$("#elementId").removeClass("oldClass");

// Modifying attributes
$("#elementId").attr("src", "new-image.jpg");

// Changing CSS styles
$("#elementId").css("color", "blue");
```

- **Event Handling:**

```
// Handling a click event
$("#buttonId").click(function() {
  // Your code here
});
```

```
// Handling a hover event
$("#elementId").hover(
  function() {
    // Mouse enters element
  },
  function() {
    // Mouse leaves element
  }
);
```

7.2.5 When to Use jQuery

While jQuery remains a valuable tool, consider these factors when deciding whether to use it:

- **Project Requirements:** For small projects or specific tasks, jQuery can be a lightweight and efficient choice.

- **Legacy Projects:** If you're maintaining or extending existing jQuery-based projects, continuing to use jQuery is practical.

- **Modern Frameworks:** For new projects and larger applications, modern front-end frameworks like React, Vue, or Angular may offer more robust solutions.

jQuery's simplicity and versatility make it a valuable asset for DOM manipulation and event handling in web development. While it coexists alongside more modern front-end frameworks, jQuery remains a practical choice for various scenarios, particularly when dealing with legacy code or smaller projects where lightweight solutions are preferred. In the following sections of this chapter, we'll explore these modern front-end frameworks in more detail, helping you choose the right tool for your web development needs.

7.3 Bootstrap for Responsive Web Design

Responsive web design is crucial in today's digital landscape, as users access websites on a variety of devices and screen sizes. Bootstrap, a popular front-end framework, offers a robust set of tools and components that simplify the process of creating responsive web designs. In this section, we'll explore how Bootstrap can be used to achieve responsive web layouts and enhance user experiences.

7.3.1 Introduction to Bootstrap

Bootstrap is an open-source front-end framework developed by Twitter. It provides a comprehensive set of HTML, CSS, and JavaScript components, along with a responsive grid system, that enables developers to create visually appealing and responsive web designs quickly.

7.3.2 Key Features of Bootstrap

Bootstrap offers a wide range of features and components that contribute to responsive web design:

- **Responsive Grid System:** Bootstrap's grid system is based on a 12-column layout that adjusts fluidly to different screen sizes. It allows developers to create responsive and mobile-friendly layouts with ease.

- **Pre-Designed UI Components:** Bootstrap includes a collection of UI components such as navigation bars, buttons, forms, modals, and alerts, making it easy to add interactive elements to web pages.

- **Typography and Styling:** Bootstrap provides a consistent typographic baseline and a set of predefined styles for headings, paragraphs, and other HTML elements.

- **Responsive CSS Classes:** Bootstrap offers CSS classes that control the visibility or styling of elements based on screen size, making it simple to hide, show, or reposition content for different devices.

- **JavaScript Plugins:** Bootstrap comes with JavaScript plugins like carousels, tooltips, popovers, and modals that enhance user interactions and functionality.

7.3.3 Achieving Responsive Web Design with Bootstrap

Bootstrap's responsive design capabilities can be harnessed using these techniques:

- **Grid System:** Developers can create responsive layouts by utilizing Bootstrap's grid system. This involves defining columns and their proportions for different screen sizes using classes like `.col-md-6` (for medium-sized screens) or `.col-lg-4` (for large screens).

- **Responsive Typography:** Bootstrap offers responsive font sizes and line heights that adapt to various screen sizes, ensuring legibility and aesthetics on all devices.

- **Media Queries:** Bootstrap employs media queries to define styles for different screen sizes and breakpoints, ensuring that the layout and content adapt smoothly as the screen size changes.

- **Responsive Navigation:** Bootstrap provides navigation components like the responsive navbar, which automatically collapses into a mobile-friendly menu on smaller screens.

- **Fluid Images:** Images within Bootstrap can be made responsive by adding the `.img-fluid` class, ensuring they scale appropriately on different devices.

7.3.4 Customizing Bootstrap

While Bootstrap provides a robust set of default styles and components, it is also highly customizable. Developers can tailor Bootstrap to match the unique design requirements of their projects by using Bootstrap's customization options, SASS variables, and custom CSS.

7.3.5 Advantages of Using Bootstrap

Bootstrap offers several advantages for responsive web design:

- **Rapid Development:** It accelerates development by providing ready-to-use components and responsive grid layouts.

- **Consistency:** Bootstrap enforces a consistent design language and structure across web applications, ensuring a cohesive user experience.

- **Community and Documentation:** It has a vast community of users and extensive documentation, making it easy to find solutions to common problems.

- **Cross-Browser Compatibility:** Bootstrap addresses cross-browser compatibility issues, ensuring that web applications work smoothly on different browsers.

Bootstrap is a versatile and powerful front-end framework that simplifies the implementation of responsive web design. By leveraging its responsive grid system, pre-designed UI components, and responsive CSS classes, web developers can create web applications that adapt seamlessly to various screen sizes and devices.

7.4 Integrating Third-Party Libraries

In modern web development, it's common to rely on third-party libraries to enhance functionality, save development time, and improve user experiences. In this section, we'll explore the process of integrating third-party libraries into your web projects and discuss best practices for doing so effectively.

7.4.1 The Role of Third-Party Libraries

Third-party libraries are pre-built packages of code, often open-source, that provide specific functionalities or features. They can range from JavaScript libraries and frameworks to CSS libraries and UI component libraries. Integrating these libraries into your web projects can significantly enhance your development process and the end-user experience.

7.4.2 Types of Third-Party Libraries

There are various types of third-party libraries available for different purposes:

- **JavaScript Libraries and Frameworks:** These include jQuery for DOM manipulation, D3.js for data visualization, Axios for HTTP requests, and moment.js for date and time handling.

- **UI Component Libraries:** Libraries like Material-UI, Ant Design, and Semantic UI offer pre-designed UI components and styles to improve the visual appeal and consistency of your web applications.

- **CSS Frameworks:** Libraries such as Bulma and Foundation provide CSS frameworks that streamline responsive web design and layout.

- **Charting Libraries:** Libraries like Chart.js and Highcharts simplify the creation of interactive charts and graphs.

7.4.3 Benefits of Using Third-Party Libraries

Integrating third-party libraries into your projects offers several advantages:

- **Time Savings:** Third-party libraries can save you development time by providing pre-built solutions for common tasks and features.

- **Functionality:** Libraries often offer specialized functionalities that might be challenging or time-consuming to develop from scratch.

- **Quality:** Many popular libraries are well-maintained, thoroughly tested, and have large user communities, ensuring high-quality code.

- **Cross-Browser Compatibility:** Third-party libraries often address cross-browser compatibility issues, ensuring consistent behavior across various browsers.

- **Community Support:** Libraries typically have active communities, which means access to documentation, tutorials, and support forums.

7.4.4 The Process of Integrating Third-Party Libraries

Integrating third-party libraries into your web project involves a few key steps:

- **Selection:** Choose the appropriate library based on your project's requirements and objectives. Consider factors like functionality, documentation, community support, and licensing.

- **Installation:** Depending on the library, you may need to download and include the library files in your project or use package managers like npm or Yarn to install them.

- **Initialization:** Initialize the library in your project by importing or including its JavaScript and CSS files. Follow the library's documentation for proper initialization and configuration.

- **Usage:** Utilize the library's functions, components, or styles as needed in your project. Refer to the library's documentation and examples to understand how to use it effectively.

- **Maintenance:** Regularly update the library to the latest version to benefit from bug fixes, performance improvements, and new features. Be mindful of potential breaking changes when updating.

7.4.5 Best Practices for Integrating Libraries

To ensure a smooth integration process, consider these best practices:

- **Read Documentation:** Thoroughly read the library's documentation to understand how it works, its API, and any potential caveats.

- **Check for Updates:** Keep your libraries up to date to benefit from improvements and security fixes.

- **Consider Bundle Size:** Be mindful of the size of the libraries you include, as larger bundles can lead to slower page load times.

- **Minimize Dependencies:** Limit the number of third-party libraries you rely on to reduce complexity and potential conflicts.

- **Test and Debug:** Test the integration thoroughly and be prepared to debug any issues that may arise.

Integrating third-party libraries into your web development projects is a common practice that can greatly enhance your efficiency and the quality of your applications. By carefully selecting, integrating, and maintaining third-party libraries, you can leverage the collective expertise of the development community to create feature-rich, performant, and visually appealing web applications.

Chapter 8: Web Development Best Practices

8.1 Code Organization and Maintainability

Efficient code organization and maintainability are fundamental aspects of successful web development. In this section, we'll explore best practices and strategies for

166

structuring your HTML, CSS, and JavaScript code to enhance maintainability and collaboration within your development team.

8.1.1 The Importance of Code Organization

Code organization refers to the structuring and arrangement of your codebase to improve readability, maintainability, and collaboration. Well-organized code ensures that developers can work cohesively on a project, easily understand the codebase, and make updates without introducing errors.

8.1.2 Structuring HTML Code

Organizing your HTML code effectively is crucial for creating clean and maintainable web pages:

- **Use Semantic HTML:** Employ semantic HTML elements like `<header>`, `<nav>`, `<section>`, and `<footer>` to convey the structure and meaning of your content. Semantic elements make it easier for both developers and assistive technologies to understand your page's layout.

- **Indentation and Formatting:** Maintain consistent indentation and formatting throughout your HTML code. This makes it more readable and helps identify nesting levels.

- **Comments:** Add comments to your HTML code to explain complex sections or provide context for other developers. Comments should be concise and informative.

- **Separate Structure and Presentation:** Keep the structure (HTML) separate from the presentation (CSS). Avoid using inline styles, and instead apply CSS classes to elements for styling.

8.1.3 Structuring CSS Code

Organizing your CSS code is essential for managing styles efficiently:

- **Use a CSS Preprocessor:** Consider using a CSS preprocessor like SASS or LESS to enhance code organization through features like variables, nesting, and mixins.

- **Modular CSS:** Divide your CSS into separate files or modules, each responsible for a specific part of your application. This approach makes it easier to locate and maintain styles.

- **BEM Methodology:** Adopt methodologies like BEM (Block, Element, Modifier) to create a consistent naming convention for CSS classes, improving code clarity and maintainability.

- **Order of Styles:** Establish a consistent order for your CSS properties (e.g., grouping related properties together). This makes it easier to find and update styles.

8.1.4 Structuring JavaScript Code

Structuring JavaScript code is crucial for maintainability and collaboration:

- **Modularization:** Break your JavaScript code into modules, each addressing a specific feature or functionality. This promotes code reusability and makes it easier to manage dependencies.

- **Use Functions:** Organize code logic into functions with descriptive names. Avoid long, complex functions that perform multiple tasks.

- **Avoid Global Scope:** Minimize the use of global variables and functions to prevent naming conflicts and improve encapsulation.

- **Comments and Documentation:** Document your JavaScript code with comments to explain the purpose of functions, their parameters, and expected behavior.

- **Linting:** Use a code linter like ESLint to enforce coding standards and catch potential issues early in the development process.

8.1.5 Version Control and Collaboration

Effective code organization extends to how your team collaborates on projects:

169

- **Version Control:** Implement a version control system (e.g., Git) to track changes, collaborate seamlessly, and maintain a history of code revisions.

- **Code Reviews:** Conduct regular code reviews within your team to ensure code quality, adherence to standards, and knowledge sharing.

- **Project Structure:** Establish a consistent project structure that includes directories for HTML, CSS, JavaScript, images, and other assets. This simplifies onboarding for new team members.

8.1.6 Continuous Improvement

Code organization and maintainability are ongoing efforts. Regularly revisit and refactor your codebase to keep it clean and efficient. Encourage a culture of continuous improvement within your development team.

Effective code organization and maintainability are essential practices in web development. Structuring your HTML, CSS, and JavaScript code thoughtfully, adopting naming conventions, documenting code, and collaborating through version control and code reviews are key steps toward building maintainable and scalable web applications. By following these best practices, you can create codebases that are not only easier to work with but also more robust and adaptable for future development.

8.2 Performance Optimization Techniques

In the competitive landscape of web development, performance optimization is a critical aspect of delivering fast, responsive, and efficient web applications. In this section, we'll explore essential performance optimization techniques that help improve the speed and overall user experience of your web projects.

8.2.1 The Importance of Performance Optimization

Performance optimization in web development is all about making web applications load faster, respond quicker, and use fewer resources. Faster-loading websites not only improve user satisfaction but also positively impact search engine rankings and user engagement.

8.2.2 Techniques for Performance Optimization

Here are key techniques for optimizing the performance of your web applications:

Minification and Compression

- **JavaScript and CSS Minification:** Minify your JavaScript and CSS files by removing whitespace, comments, and unnecessary characters. This reduces file sizes and speeds up downloading.

- **Compression:** Enable server-side compression, typically using Gzip or Brotli, to further reduce the size of text-based assets like HTML, CSS, and JavaScript.

Image Optimization

- **Image Formats:** Choose appropriate image formats (e.g., JPEG, PNG, WebP) and compress images to reduce file sizes without compromising quality.

- **Lazy Loading:** Implement lazy loading for images, especially for those below the fold, so they load only when users scroll to them.

- **Responsive Images:** Serve different image sizes based on the user's device and viewport, using the `<picture>` element or responsive design techniques.

Browser Caching

- **Cache Control Headers:** Configure cache control headers (e.g., Cache-Control and Expires) on your server to instruct browsers to cache static assets. This reduces server load and speeds up page loads for returning visitors.

Content Delivery Networks (CDNs)

- **CDN Integration:** Use a Content Delivery Network (CDN) to distribute your website's assets across multiple servers located in different geographic regions.

CDNs can deliver content from the nearest server, reducing latency.

Code Splitting

- **JavaScript Code Splitting:** Employ code splitting techniques to split your JavaScript into smaller chunks, loading only the necessary code for the current page or interaction. This reduces initial load times.

Efficient JavaScript

- **Optimized JavaScript:** Write efficient JavaScript code by avoiding unnecessary loops, reducing DOM manipulations, and minimizing costly operations.

- **Async and Defer Attributes:** Use the `async` and `defer` attributes when including JavaScript files to control how they load and execute, ensuring they don't block the rendering of your page.

Critical Rendering Path Optimization

- **Above-the-Fold Content:** Prioritize rendering above-the-fold content, ensuring that crucial content loads quickly and efficiently. Use asynchronous loading for non-essential resources.

Responsive Design and Media Queries

- **Media Queries:** Use media queries to apply responsive design principles, serving different layouts and assets for different screen sizes and devices.

Performance Monitoring and Testing

- **Web Performance Testing Tools:** Utilize performance testing tools like Google PageSpeed Insights, Lighthouse, or WebPageTest to identify performance bottlenecks and areas for improvement.

- **Real-User Monitoring (RUM):** Implement RUM tools to collect data on how real users experience your website. This data can inform ongoing optimization efforts.

Server-Side Optimization

- **Server Resources:** Ensure your web server has adequate resources (CPU, RAM, etc.) to handle traffic efficiently. Consider using load balancing and auto-scaling for high-traffic websites.

Content Delivery Optimization

- **Content Delivery:** Serve static assets from cookieless domains or subdomains to reduce the overhead of sending unnecessary cookies with each request.

Progressive Web Apps (PWAs)

- **PWAs:** Consider turning your web application into a Progressive Web App (PWA) to provide a fast and reliable user experience, even in low-network conditions.

8.2.3 Continuous Monitoring and Improvement

Web performance is an ongoing concern. Regularly monitor your website's performance metrics, gather user feedback, and make improvements based on data and user behavior.

Performance optimization is a critical aspect of web development that directly impacts user satisfaction and website success. By applying these optimization techniques and staying vigilant about web performance, you can ensure that your web applications load quickly, respond efficiently, and deliver an exceptional user experience. Embracing performance optimization as a fundamental practice will set your web development projects on a path to success in today's competitive online landscape.

8.3 Cross-Browser Compatibility

Cross-browser compatibility is a critical aspect of web development, ensuring that websites and web applications function consistently and correctly across various web browsers. In this section, we'll explore the importance of cross-browser compatibility and best practices for achieving it.

8.3.1 The Significance of Cross-Browser Compatibility

Cross-browser compatibility refers to a web application's ability to work correctly and consistently across different web browsers, including popular options like Google Chrome,

Mozilla Firefox, Microsoft Edge, Safari, and others. Achieving cross-browser compatibility is crucial for several reasons:

- **User Experience:** Users access websites using various browsers and devices. Inconsistent experiences can lead to frustration and deter users from returning to your site.

- **Market Share:** Different browsers have varying market shares in different regions and among different demographics. Ensuring compatibility maximizes your potential audience.

- **SEO and Rankings:** Search engines consider user experience when ranking websites. Cross-browser compatibility can indirectly impact your site's search engine rankings.

- **Brand Reputation:** A website that works well across browsers reflects positively on your brand's professionalism and attention to detail.

8.3.2 Challenges in Cross-Browser Compatibility

Achieving cross-browser compatibility can be challenging due to the following factors:

- **Differing Rendering Engines:** Browsers use different rendering engines (e.g., Blink, Gecko, WebKit) to interpret and display web content. Each engine may interpret HTML, CSS, and JavaScript slightly differently.

- **Vendor-Specific Features:** Browsers may implement proprietary features or CSS properties, leading to inconsistencies in rendering.

- **Version Differences:** Within the same browser, different versions may behave differently. Older versions may not support modern web technologies or standards.

8.3.3 Best Practices for Cross-Browser Compatibility

To ensure cross-browser compatibility, follow these best practices:

Validate HTML and CSS

- **HTML Validation:** Validate your HTML code using tools like the W3C Markup Validation Service to ensure compliance with web standards.

- **CSS Validation:** Validate your CSS code using services like the W3C CSS Validation Service to catch syntax errors and potential issues.

Use Modern Web Standards

- **HTML5 and CSS3:** Embrace modern web standards and features provided by HTML5 and CSS3, but be aware of browser support and provide fallbacks when necessary.

Feature Detection and Progressive Enhancement

- **Feature Detection:** Use JavaScript to detect whether a browser supports a particular feature before attempting to use it. Libraries like Modernizr can help with feature detection.

- **Progressive Enhancement:** Start with a solid, basic experience and progressively enhance it for browsers that support advanced features.

Normalize and Reset CSS

- **CSS Reset:** Use a CSS reset or normalize stylesheet to level the playing field, reducing browser-specific default styles.

Cross-Browser Testing

- **Testing Matrix:** Test your website or application on a variety of browsers and versions. Prioritize testing on browsers with the highest user base for your target audience.

- **Browser Developer Tools:** Familiarize yourself with browser developer tools for debugging and testing.

- **Online Services:** Utilize online services that offer browser testing across multiple platforms and versions.

Polyfills and Shims

- **Polyfills:** Use polyfills (JavaScript libraries that provide modern functionality in older browsers) to bridge compatibility gaps.

- **Shims:** Consider using shims (small code snippets) to provide missing functionality in older browsers.

Documentation

- **Browser Support Documentation:** Maintain clear documentation that outlines which browsers and versions are officially supported by your website or application.

Regular Updates

- **Stay Informed:** Keep up with browser updates and changes in web standards. Adjust your codebase accordingly to address compatibility issues as they arise.

Cross-browser compatibility is a fundamental aspect of web development that ensures a seamless user experience across diverse web environments. By adhering to best practices, conducting thorough testing, and staying informed about web standards and browser updates, you can ensure that your websites and web applications are accessible and functional for users, regardless of the browser they choose to use. Prioritizing cross-browser compatibility is key to building a successful online presence and maintaining a positive brand image in the digital world.

8.4 SEO Best Practices

Search Engine Optimization (SEO) is a crucial aspect of web development that focuses on improving a website's visibility in search engine results pages. In this section, we'll explore SEO best practices that can help your website rank higher in search engine results and attract organic traffic.

8.4.1 The Significance of SEO

SEO plays a vital role in web development for several reasons:

- **Increased Visibility:** High search engine rankings mean your website is more likely to be seen by users searching for relevant content or products.

- **Organic Traffic:** SEO efforts can drive organic (unpaid) traffic to your site, reducing the need for paid advertising.

- **User Experience:** SEO practices often align with good user experience, making your website more user-friendly and accessible.

8.4.2 SEO Best Practices

To improve your website's SEO, follow these best practices:

Keyword Research

- **Keyword Selection:** Identify relevant keywords and phrases that your target audience is likely to search for. Use tools like Google Keyword Planner to discover popular keywords.

- **Long-Tail Keywords:** Consider using long-tail keywords (more specific, longer phrases) to target niche audiences.

On-Page SEO

- **Title Tags:** Include unique and descriptive title tags for each page. Place important keywords near the beginning.

- **Meta Descriptions:** Write compelling meta descriptions that summarize the content of each page. Include relevant keywords.

- **Header Tags:** Use header tags (H1, H2, H3, etc.) to structure your content and make it more readable. Include keywords in headers where appropriate.

- **Image Alt Text:** Add descriptive alt text to images to improve accessibility and provide search engines with context.

- **URL Structure:** Create clean and descriptive URLs that include keywords where relevant.

- **Internal Linking:** Include internal links to other relevant pages on your website to improve navigation and encourage users to explore more content.

High-Quality Content

- **Original Content:** Create high-quality, original content that provides value to your audience. Avoid duplicate content.

- **Keyword Usage:** Naturally incorporate keywords into your content, but avoid keyword stuffing (overusing keywords unnaturally).

- **Regular Updates:** Consistently update your website with fresh content to keep users engaged and encourage search engines to crawl your site frequently.

Mobile-Friendly Design

- **Responsive Design:** Ensure your website is mobile-responsive, meaning it adapts to different screen sizes and devices. Google prioritizes mobile-friendly websites in its rankings.

Page Load Speed

- **Optimize Images:** Compress and optimize images to reduce page load times.

- **Minify Code:** Minimize and compress HTML, CSS, and JavaScript files to improve loading speed.

User Experience (UX)

- **Mobile Usability:** Ensure mobile users have a smooth and intuitive experience on your site.

- **Readability:** Use legible fonts and maintain good contrast for text readability.

Technical SEO

- **XML Sitemap:** Create an XML sitemap to help search engines index your pages more efficiently.

- **Robots.txt:** Use a robots.txt file to control which pages search engines can and cannot crawl.

- **SSL Certificate:** Secure your website with an SSL certificate to provide a secure browsing experience.

Backlinks and Off-Page SEO

- **Backlink Building:** Acquire high-quality backlinks from reputable websites in your industry.

- **Social Media:** Maintain an active presence on social media platforms to promote your content and attract visitors.

Analytics and Monitoring

- **Google Analytics:** Use tools like Google Analytics to track website traffic, user behavior, and the effectiveness of your SEO efforts.

SEO is a dynamic and ongoing process that requires careful planning and consistent effort. By implementing these SEO best practices in your web development projects, you can increase your website's visibility, attract organic traffic, and provide a better user experience. Remember that SEO is not a one-time task but rather an integral part of your web development strategy that should evolve as search engine algorithms and user behavior change.

8.5 Web Accessibility Considerations

Web accessibility, often referred to as a11y (a for accessibility and 11 for the 11 letters between "a" and "y"), is a critical aspect of web development that focuses on ensuring that websites and web applications are usable by people with disabilities. In this section, we'll explore the importance of web accessibility and best practices for creating inclusive digital experiences.

8.5.1 The Significance of Web Accessibility

Web accessibility is essential for several reasons:

- **Inclusivity:** Web accessibility ensures that individuals with disabilities can access and interact with online content, products, and services on an equal basis with others.

- **Legal Requirements:** Many countries have laws and regulations that require websites and web applications to be accessible to people with disabilities. Non-compliance can result in legal consequences.

- **User Base:** Millions of people worldwide have disabilities that affect their online experiences, including those with visual, auditory, motor, or cognitive impairments.

- **Improved User Experience:** Web accessibility practices often benefit all users by enhancing usability and clarity.

8.5.2 Web Accessibility Best Practices

To create accessible web content, consider the following best practices:

Semantic HTML

- **Use Semantic Elements:** Employ semantic HTML elements (e.g., `<button>`, `<input>`, `<h1>`, `<nav>`) to convey the meaning and structure of your content. Avoid using non-semantic elements like `<div>` for interactive elements.

- **Proper Headings:** Use hierarchical heading elements (`<h1>` to `<h6>`) to structure your content logically. Headings should describe the content that follows and help screen reader users navigate.

Alternative Text for Images

- **Alt Text:** Provide descriptive alt text for all images. Alt text should convey the purpose and content of an image, ensuring that screen reader users can understand it.

Keyboard Accessibility

- **Keyboard Navigation:** Ensure that all interactive elements, including links, buttons, and form fields, can be accessed and operated using a keyboard alone. Avoid relying on mouse-only actions.

Focus Management

- **Focus Indicator:** Make sure that keyboard focus is visible and clearly distinguishable. Users should be able to see which element currently has focus.

- **Skip Links:** Implement skip links that allow users to bypass repetitive navigation menus and jump directly to the main content.

Forms and Labels

- **Labels for Form Fields:** Always associate form fields with descriptive labels. Labels provide context and clarity for all users.

- **Error Messages:** Clearly communicate error messages and validation requirements to users, especially those using screen readers or keyboard navigation.

Text Alternatives for Multimedia

- **Transcripts:** Provide transcripts for audio and video content to make multimedia accessible to users with hearing impairments.

ARIA (Accessible Rich Internet Applications)

- **ARIA Roles and Attributes:** Use ARIA roles and attributes to enhance the accessibility of dynamic and interactive content, such as single-page applications.

Testing and User Feedback

- **Accessibility Testing:** Regularly test your website or application for accessibility using automated tools, manual testing, and assistive technologies.

- **User Feedback:** Seek feedback from users with disabilities to identify and address accessibility issues.

8.5.3 Compliance with Standards

- **Web Content Accessibility Guidelines (WCAG):** Familiarize yourself with the WCAG, a set of internationally recognized guidelines for web accessibility. Strive to meet the WCAG criteria, which are organized into three levels of conformance: A, AA, and AAA.

Web accessibility is a moral, legal, and user-centric imperative in web development. By implementing web accessibility best practices in your projects, you can create digital experiences that are inclusive and beneficial to all users, regardless of their abilities. Prioritizing accessibility not only aligns with ethical standards but also contributes to a more welcoming and diverse online environment.

Chapter 9: Deployment and Hosting

Congratulations, you've reached a pivotal stage in your web development journey—deployment and hosting. You've invested time and effort into creating a fantastic web application, and now it's time to share it with the world. In this chapter, we'll explore the intricate process of taking your web project from your local development environment to a live server accessible to anyone with an internet connection.

Deployment and hosting are crucial aspects of web development that can significantly impact the accessibility, performance, and reliability of your website or web application. Whether you're building a personal blog, an e-commerce platform, or a cutting-edge web app, the principles of deployment and hosting apply across the board.

We'll guide you through the key concepts and best practices of deploying your HTML, CSS, and JavaScript projects, ensuring that your creation reaches its full potential. You'll discover the various hosting options available, from shared hosting to cloud services, and learn how to choose the one that best suits your needs.

9.1 Choosing a Web Hosting Service

When it comes to deploying your web project and making it accessible to the world, choosing the right web hosting service is a critical decision. Your hosting provider plays a significant role in determining the performance, reliability, and security of your website or web application. In this section, we'll explore the factors to consider when selecting a web hosting service that best suits your needs.

9.1.1 Types of Web Hosting Services

Before diving into the selection process, it's essential to understand the various types of web hosting services available:

Shared Hosting

- **Overview:** Shared hosting is an affordable option where multiple websites share the same server resources. It's suitable for small websites and personal blogs with low traffic.

- **Pros:** Cost-effective, easy to set up, and ideal for beginners.

- **Cons:** Limited resources, reduced performance during traffic spikes, and potential security risks if one site on the server is compromised.

Virtual Private Server (VPS) Hosting

- **Overview:** VPS hosting provides a dedicated virtual server within a shared physical server. It offers more control and resources than shared hosting.

- **Pros:** Better performance, customization options, and increased security compared to shared hosting.

- **Cons:** Requires more technical expertise, and server management is typically the user's responsibility.

Dedicated Server Hosting

- **Overview:** With dedicated server hosting, you get an entire physical server dedicated to your website or application. It offers the highest level of control and resources.

- **Pros:** Maximum performance, complete control over server configuration, and enhanced security.

- **Cons:** Expensive, requires advanced server administration skills, and may be overkill for small websites.

Cloud Hosting

- **Overview:** Cloud hosting distributes your website across a network of virtual servers, ensuring scalability and reliability. You pay for the resources you use.

- **Pros:** Scalability, high availability, and pay-as-you-go pricing.

- **Cons:** Pricing can be complex, and advanced configurations may require technical expertise.

Managed WordPress Hosting

- **Overview:** Managed WordPress hosting is specialized for WordPress websites, offering optimized performance and security. Providers handle server maintenance.

- **Pros:** Ideal for WordPress users, excellent performance, and automated updates.

- **Cons:** Limited to WordPress sites, may be costlier than traditional shared hosting.

9.1.2 Factors to Consider

When choosing a web hosting service, consider the following factors:

Hosting Needs

- **Traffic:** Estimate your expected website traffic. Different hosting types handle traffic differently.

- **Resource Requirements:** Assess your resource needs, including CPU, RAM, storage, and bandwidth.

- **Technical Expertise:** Evaluate your technical skills for server management and maintenance.

Performance and Reliability

- **Uptime Guarantee:** Look for hosting providers with a high uptime guarantee (99.9% or higher).

- **Server Locations:** Choose servers located geographically close to your target audience for faster load times.

- **Scalability:** Ensure your hosting plan allows for easy scalability as your website grows.

Security

- **Security Features:** Check for security features like SSL certificates, firewalls, and regular backups.

- **Updates and Patching:** Ensure the hosting provider keeps server software up to date.

- **DDoS Protection:** Assess the level of protection against Distributed Denial of Service (DDoS) attacks.

Support and Customer Service

- **24/7 Support:** Opt for a provider with round-the-clock customer support.

- **Support Channels:** Consider the availability of support channels (live chat, email, phone).

Pricing and Billing

- **Cost Structure:** Understand the pricing model (e.g., monthly, annually) and any hidden fees.

- **Scalability:** Check if you can easily upgrade or downgrade your hosting plan.

User Reviews and Recommendations

- **Research:** Read reviews and seek recommendations from peers or online communities.

Choosing the right web hosting service is a crucial decision that can impact the performance, security, and scalability of your website or web application. By carefully assessing your needs and considering factors like hosting type, performance, security, support, pricing, and user feedback, you can make an informed choice that aligns with your project's goals.

Remember that your hosting provider should be a reliable partner in your web development journey, supporting your success as your online presence grows.

9.2 Uploading Your Website

Once you've chosen the right web hosting service for your project, the next crucial step is uploading your website or web application to the hosting server. This process ensures that your carefully crafted HTML, CSS, and JavaScript files are accessible to users across the internet. In this section, we'll guide you through the steps to upload your website successfully.

9.2.1 Preparing Your Files

Before you start the upload process, make sure you've prepared your website files:

- **File Organization:** Organize your website files into a structured directory. It's common to have a main directory containing HTML, CSS, JavaScript, and other assets like images and videos.

- **File Optimization:** Optimize your website assets for performance by compressing images, minifying CSS and JavaScript, and eliminating unnecessary files.

- **Backup:** Create a backup of your website files in case anything goes wrong during the upload.

9.2.2 Accessing Your Hosting Account

To upload your files to the hosting server, you'll typically use one of the following methods:

FTP (File Transfer Protocol)

- **Overview:** FTP is a common method for uploading files to a web server. You'll need FTP software like FileZilla or Cyberduck.

- **Access Details:** Obtain your FTP server address, username, and password from your hosting provider.

- **File Transfer:** Connect to the server using your FTP client, navigate to the destination folder (usually the public_html or www folder), and upload your website files.

Control Panel File Manager

- **Overview:** Many hosting providers offer a web-based control panel (e.g., cPanel, Plesk) with a built-in file manager.

- **Access Details:** Log in to your hosting control panel using the provided credentials.

- **File Transfer:** Use the file manager to navigate to the public_html or www directory and upload your website files directly from your local computer.

Git Repository Deployment

- **Overview:** If your website is managed using version control (e.g., Git), you can set up deployment pipelines that automatically push changes to your hosting server when you commit to a specific branch.

- **Access Details:** Configure your hosting provider's integration with your Git repository.

- **Continuous Deployment:** Whenever you commit changes to the designated branch, they will be automatically deployed to your hosting server.

9.2.3 Domain Configuration

After uploading your website files, you'll need to configure your domain name to point to your hosting server. This step ensures that visitors can access your site using a user-friendly domain name (e.g., www.yourwebsite.com).

- **Domain Registration:** If you haven't registered a domain, you can do so through your hosting provider or a domain registrar.

- **Domain DNS Settings:** Access your domain's DNS settings and update the name servers provided by your hosting provider. This step may take some time to propagate across the internet.

9.2.4 Testing and Troubleshooting

After uploading your website and configuring your domain, thoroughly test your website to ensure everything is working as expected. Pay attention to issues like broken links, missing assets, and functionality problems.

- **Browser Testing:** Check your website in various web browsers to ensure cross-browser compatibility.

- **Mobile Responsiveness:** Verify that your website is responsive and displays correctly on different devices and screen sizes.

- **Forms and Functionality:** Test interactive elements like forms, buttons, and scripts to confirm they work correctly.

- **SSL Certificate:** If your hosting plan includes SSL (Secure Sockets Layer), ensure that your website loads over HTTPS with a valid SSL certificate.

- **Performance:** Use website performance testing tools to assess page load times and identify areas for improvement.

If you encounter any issues, review error logs, and consult your hosting provider's support resources or customer support for assistance.

Uploading your website to a hosting server is a crucial step in making your web project accessible to users worldwide. By properly preparing your files, selecting the appropriate upload method, configuring your domain, and conducting thorough testing, you can ensure a smooth deployment process. Remember that the deployment phase is not the end of your web development journey but rather the beginning of sharing your creation with the online community.

9.3 Domain Name Configuration

Configuring your domain name is a critical step in the deployment and hosting process. Your domain name is your website's unique address on the internet, and configuring it correctly ensures that users can access your website using a user-friendly and memorable URL. In this section, we'll explore the domain name configuration process and provide guidance on setting up your domain effectively.

9.3.1 Domain Registration

Before configuring your domain, you need to register it with a domain registrar. Domain registration is the process of reserving a unique internet address for your website. Here's what you need to do:

- **Choose a Domain Registrar:** Select a reputable domain registrar to register your domain name. Popular registrars include GoDaddy, Namecheap, Google Domains, and many others.

- **Search for Availability:** Use the registrar's search tool to check if your desired domain name is available. If it is, you can proceed with registration.

- **Provide Information:** During registration, you'll be asked to provide contact information and create an account with the registrar.

- **Select Domain Period:** Choose the duration for which you want to register the domain (e.g., one year, multiple years).

- **Make Payment:** Complete the registration process by making the required payment.

9.3.2 DNS (Domain Name System) Configuration

DNS configuration allows you to map your domain name to the IP address of your hosting server. When users enter your domain in a web browser, the DNS system directs them to the correct server where your website is hosted. Here's how to configure DNS:

- **Access DNS Settings:** Log in to your domain registrar's control panel or dashboard, locate the domain you've registered, and look for DNS settings or DNS management.

- **Update Name Servers:** In the DNS settings, update the name servers to those provided by your hosting provider. These name servers will point to the hosting server where your website files are stored.

- **Propagation Time:** Keep in mind that DNS changes may take some time to propagate across the internet. It can vary from minutes to 48 hours, depending on various factors and DNS caching.

9.3.3 Domain Redirects and Subdomains

Depending on your website's structure and goals, you might want to configure domain redirects or set up subdomains:

- **Domain Redirects:** You can set up domain redirects to forward users from one domain to another. This is useful for consolidating multiple domains or handling changes in your website's structure.

- **Subdomains:** Subdomains allow you to create separate sections or microsites within your main domain. For example, you can have blog.yourwebsite.com for your blog or shop.yourwebsite.com for your e-commerce store.

9.3.4 SSL/TLS Certificates

For security and trustworthiness, consider configuring an SSL/TLS certificate for your domain. SSL (Secure Sockets Layer) or TLS (Transport Layer Security) encrypts data exchanged between the user's browser and your server. Many hosting providers offer free SSL certificates, which can be

201

installed easily through your hosting control panel or dashboard.

9.3.5 Testing and Troubleshooting

After configuring your domain, it's essential to thoroughly test your website to ensure that it loads correctly and securely using your domain name. Check for any issues, such as broken links or mixed content warnings (HTTP resources on an HTTPS page), and resolve them promptly.

Domain name configuration is a crucial step in making your website accessible to users via a user-friendly and memorable URL. By registering your domain, configuring DNS settings, setting up domain redirects or subdomains as needed, and ensuring secure connections with SSL/TLS certificates, you can establish a strong online presence. Effective domain configuration not only enhances your website's accessibility but also contributes to its professionalism and trustworthiness in the eyes of your visitors.

9.4 SSL/TLS Security

SSL (Secure Sockets Layer) and its successor TLS (Transport Layer Security) are cryptographic protocols that provide secure communication over the internet. Implementing SSL/TLS security for your website is crucial in today's digital landscape. In this section, we'll explore SSL/TLS security and why it's essential for your deployed web projects.

9.4.1 What is SSL/TLS?

SSL/TLS is a security protocol that encrypts data transmitted between a user's web browser and the web server. It ensures that sensitive information, such as login credentials, credit card numbers, and personal data, remains private and secure during transmission. SSL/TLS operates as a layer between the application layer (where your website functions) and the transport layer (where data is transmitted).

9.4.2 The Importance of SSL/TLS Security

Implementing SSL/TLS security offers several crucial benefits:

- **Data Encryption:** SSL/TLS encrypts data, making it unreadable to unauthorized parties. Even if intercepted, the data remains confidential.

- **Authentication:** SSL/TLS provides authentication, ensuring users connect to the legitimate server and not an imposter.

- **Trust and Credibility:** Websites with SSL/TLS certificates display a padlock icon in the browser's address bar and use "https://" in their URLs. These visual cues signal trust to users.

- **Search Engine Ranking:** Major search engines like Google prioritize secure websites in search rankings. SSL/TLS is a ranking factor, meaning it can improve your website's visibility.

9.4.3 Obtaining an SSL/TLS Certificate

To enable SSL/TLS security for your website, you'll need to obtain an SSL/TLS certificate. Here's how to do it:

- **Purchase a Certificate:** You can buy SSL/TLS certificates from certificate authorities (CAs) or through your hosting provider. Some providers offer free certificates through initiatives like Let's Encrypt.

- **Generate a Certificate Signing Request (CSR):** If required, generate a CSR on your web server. This request contains information about your domain and is used to create the certificate.

- **Complete Validation:** The CA will validate your domain ownership before issuing the certificate. This typically involves email verification or adding a DNS record.

- **Install the Certificate:** Once issued, install the certificate on your web server. Most hosting providers offer tools and guides to simplify this process.

9.4.4 HTTPS Implementation

After obtaining and installing an SSL/TLS certificate, you need to configure your web server to use HTTPS (Hypertext Transfer Protocol Secure). Here's what you should do:

- **Update Server Settings:** Adjust your web server configuration to enable HTTPS. Ensure that incoming traffic is routed through the secure HTTPS protocol.

- **Mixed Content:** Ensure that all resources (images, scripts, stylesheets) loaded on your website use HTTPS. Mixed content (a combination of secure and non-secure resources) can trigger browser warnings.

9.4.5 Periodic Renewal and Monitoring

SSL/TLS certificates typically have a limited validity period (e.g., one year or two years). It's essential to renew your certificate before it expires to avoid any security issues. Many certificate providers offer automatic renewal options.

Additionally, monitor your SSL/TLS configuration regularly to ensure it remains secure. Vulnerabilities or outdated configurations can pose risks to your website's security.

SSL/TLS security is a fundamental aspect of deploying and hosting a website in today's internet landscape. It not only protects sensitive data but also instills trust and credibility in your visitors. By obtaining and configuring an SSL/TLS certificate, enabling HTTPS, and keeping your security measures up to date, you can provide a secure and reliable online experience for your users while meeting the expectations of modern web standards and search engine requirements.

9.5 Continuous Integration and Deployment (CI/CD)

Continuous Integration and Deployment, often abbreviated as CI/CD, is a set of practices and tools used in web development to automate and streamline the process of deploying web applications. In this section, we'll explore how CI/CD can improve your deployment workflow, enhance code quality, and increase the efficiency of your web development projects.

9.5.1 Understanding CI/CD

Continuous Integration (CI) and Continuous Deployment (CD) are two interconnected practices:

- **Continuous Integration (CI):** CI involves regularly integrating code changes from multiple developers into a shared repository. Automated tests are run to detect integration issues and ensure that new code doesn't break existing functionality.

- **Continuous Deployment (CD):** CD takes CI a step further by automating the deployment process. After passing CI tests, changes are automatically deployed to a staging or production environment.

9.5.2 Benefits of CI/CD in Web Development

Implementing CI/CD offers several advantages for web development projects:

- **Faster Development:** CI/CD reduces the time it takes to deploy code changes, allowing you to deliver new features and bug fixes more rapidly.

- **Consistency:** Automated deployment ensures that the same process is followed every time, reducing the risk of human error.

- **Early Issue Detection:** CI identifies code integration issues early in the development cycle, making it easier to address and preventing bugs from reaching the production environment.

- **Improved Collaboration:** CI encourages collaboration among developers by providing a shared, automated environment for integrating and testing code changes.

9.5.3 CI/CD Workflow

A typical CI/CD workflow consists of the following stages:

- **Code Commit:** Developers commit their code changes to a version control system (e.g., Git).

- **Automated Build:** CI tools automatically build the application from the committed code.

- **Automated Testing:** Automated tests, including unit tests, integration tests, and end-to-end tests, are executed to ensure code quality and functionality.

- **Artifact Generation:** Successful builds produce deployable artifacts, such as compiled code, assets, or containers.

- **Deployment to Staging:** The application is deployed to a staging environment where further testing and validation occur.

- **User Acceptance Testing (UAT):** Stakeholders, including QA teams or clients, can test the application in a staging environment.

- **Deployment to Production:** After passing all tests and receiving approval, the code changes are automatically deployed to the production environment.

- **Monitoring and Feedback:** Continuous monitoring and feedback mechanisms help detect issues in production and inform future improvements.

9.5.4 CI/CD Tools and Services

Numerous CI/CD tools and services are available to streamline the CI/CD pipeline, including Jenkins, Travis CI, CircleCI, GitLab CI/CD, and GitHub Actions. These tools automate various aspects of the workflow, from code integration to testing and deployment.

9.5.5 CI/CD in Web Hosting

Many web hosting providers offer integrations with CI/CD services, allowing you to automate deployments directly from your code repository. This seamless integration simplifies the process of deploying updates to your hosted website or web application.

CI/CD is a powerful practice that can significantly improve the efficiency, quality, and reliability of your web development projects. By automating code integration, testing, and deployment, you can reduce development cycle times, catch issues early, and deliver a seamless and responsive web experience to your users. Consider implementing CI/CD in your web development workflow to stay competitive and meet the demands of today's fast-paced digital landscape.

Chapter 10: Building a Complete Web Project

Congratulations on reaching the final chapter of this web development journey. In the preceding chapters, you've acquired the essential skills and knowledge needed to create web content using HTML, style it with CSS, and add interactivity and functionality with JavaScript. You've explored hosting, deployment, and best practices for web development.

Now, it's time to put everything together in a comprehensive, hands-on project.

Building a complete web project is a thrilling endeavor that allows you to apply your newfound skills and creativity to craft a fully functional and visually appealing website. Whether you're developing a personal portfolio, a blog, an e-commerce platform, or a dynamic web application, this chapter will guide you through the process, from conceptualization to deployment.

10.1 Planning Your Web Project

Before diving into the actual development of your web project, it's crucial to start with a well-thought-out plan. Effective planning lays the foundation for a successful project, guiding you through the design, development, and deployment phases. In this section, we'll explore the key aspects of planning your web project.

10.1.1 Defining Project Goals

Begin by defining clear and achievable goals for your web project. Ask yourself the following questions:

- **What is the purpose of this project?** Determine whether your project is meant to inform, entertain, sell products, provide services, or serve another purpose.

211

- **Who is the target audience?** Understand your audience's demographics, interests, and needs to tailor your project to their preferences.

- **What problem does the project solve?** Identify the specific issue or need your project addresses.

- **What are the desired outcomes?** Set measurable objectives to gauge the project's success. These could include metrics like website traffic, user engagement, or conversion rates.

10.1.2 Creating a Project Scope

The project scope defines the boundaries and features of your web project. It outlines what will and won't be included in your project. Consider the following:

- **Feature List:** Create a detailed list of the features and functionalities your project will offer. Prioritize them based on importance and complexity.

- **Content Structure:** Plan how your content will be organized, including the website's navigation structure and the types of content (text, images, videos) you'll use.

- **Technical Requirements:** Outline the technologies and tools you'll need to use, such as specific libraries, frameworks, or content management systems (CMS).

10.1.3 Wireframing and Mockups

Visualize the layout and design of your web project through wireframes and mockups:

- **Wireframes:** These are basic, simplified layouts that show the structure of each page without intricate design elements. Wireframes help you focus on content placement and functionality.

- **Mockups:** Mockups are detailed, visual representations of your project's pages, including colors, typography, and branding elements. They provide a clear vision of the final design.

10.1.4 Information Architecture

Determine how information will be organized and accessed on your website. This includes creating a sitemap that outlines the hierarchy of pages and their relationships. Consider user-friendly navigation and clear pathways to essential content.

10.1.5 User Experience (UX) Design

Think about the overall user experience. Focus on:

- **Navigation:** Ensure users can easily find what they're looking for.

- **Responsiveness:** Plan for a responsive design that adapts to various screen sizes and devices.

- **Accessibility:** Make your project accessible to users with disabilities by following web accessibility guidelines (WCAG).

10.1.6 Project Timeline and Milestones

Develop a timeline for your project, breaking it into milestones with specific deadlines. This helps you stay organized and on track throughout the development process.

10.1.7 Budget and Resources

Consider the resources required for your project, including tools, software licenses, hosting costs, and potential outsourcing. Create a budget to estimate and manage expenses effectively.

10.1.8 Risk Assessment

Identify potential risks that could impact your project's success. Develop mitigation strategies for each risk to minimize their impact.

10.1.9 Documentation

Keep detailed records of your project plan, including your goals, scope, wireframes, mockups, and technical specifications. Documentation helps maintain clarity and consistency throughout the project.

10.1.10 Stakeholder Communication

If your project involves collaborators or stakeholders, establish clear communication channels to keep everyone informed and aligned with project goals.

By thoroughly planning your web project, you set the stage for a smoother development process and increase the likelihood of achieving your objectives. With a well-defined plan in hand, you're ready to move on to the next phases of web development, where you'll turn your vision into a fully functional web project.

10.2 Implementing a Responsive Design

In today's digital landscape, users access websites and web applications through an array of devices, including desktop computers, laptops, tablets, and smartphones. To ensure that your web project is accessible and user-friendly across all these platforms, it's essential to implement a responsive design. In this section, we'll explore the principles and techniques of creating a responsive web design.

10.2.1 What Is Responsive Design?

Responsive web design is an approach that aims to make web content adapt seamlessly to different screen sizes and resolutions. This adaptation ensures that users have a consistent and enjoyable experience, regardless of whether they're using a large desktop monitor or a small mobile device.

10.2.2 Principles of Responsive Design

To implement responsive design effectively, keep the following principles in mind:

- **Fluid Grids:** Instead of fixed-width layouts, use fluid grids that adjust dynamically based on screen width. This allows content to flow and resize proportionally.

- **Flexible Images and Media:** Images and media should also be flexible and resize with the layout. Use CSS techniques like `max-width: 100%` to prevent images from overflowing their containers.

- **Media Queries:** Media queries are CSS rules that apply styles based on screen characteristics such as width, height, and device orientation. Use media queries to define different styles for different screen sizes or breakpoints.

- **Mobile-First Approach:** Start designing and developing for mobile devices first and then progressively enhance the experience for larger screens. This approach ensures a solid foundation for all devices.

10.2.3 Practical Techniques for Responsive Design

Here are some practical techniques to implement responsive design in your web project:

- **Viewport Meta Tag:** Include the viewport meta tag (`<meta name="viewport" content="width=device-width, initial-scale=1.0">`) in your HTML to ensure that the website adapts to the device's screen width.

- **CSS Frameworks:** Consider using CSS frameworks like Bootstrap or Foundation, which come with built-in responsive design components and grids.

- **Flexbox and Grid Layout:** CSS Flexbox and Grid Layout are powerful tools for creating responsive layouts. They allow you to arrange and align content with ease.

- **Media Queries:** As mentioned earlier, use media queries to apply different styles for various screen sizes. For example, you can adjust font sizes, margins, and even hide or show elements as needed.

- **Images and Media Optimization:** Optimize images for the web by compressing them and providing different image sizes for different screen resolutions. Use the `<picture>` element or the `srcset` attribute to serve appropriate images based on device capabilities.

- **Testing and Debugging:** Regularly test your responsive design on various devices and browsers to identify and resolve issues. Browser developer tools often include device emulation features for testing.

10.2.4 User Experience Considerations

A responsive design isn't just about adjusting layout and elements; it's also about providing an excellent user experience. Consider the following:

- **Touch-Friendly Design:** Ensure that interactive elements are easily tappable on touchscreen devices.

- **Navigation:** Simplify navigation menus for smaller screens, possibly using hamburger menus or accordion-style navigation.

- **Performance:** Optimize your web project for performance, as mobile devices may have limited processing power and slower internet connections.

- **Accessibility:** Maintain accessibility standards to accommodate users with disabilities across all devices.

Implementing a responsive design is a critical step in creating a web project that appeals to a wide audience. By following responsive design principles, using practical techniques, and considering user experience, you can ensure that your web project is accessible and user-friendly on devices of all shapes and sizes. A responsive design not only improves usability but also enhances your project's credibility and user satisfaction.

10.3 Integrating Front-End and Back-End

In the process of building a complete web project, you'll often encounter the need to integrate the front-end and back-end components seamlessly. The front-end represents the user interface and client-side functionality, while the back-end handles server-side operations and data management. In this section, we'll explore the importance of integrating these two aspects of web development and discuss the strategies for achieving a cohesive and functional web project.

10.3.1 The Front-End and Back-End Divide

Front-end and back-end development are distinct yet interconnected aspects of web development:

- **Front-End:** This includes the user interface (UI) and the client-side logic responsible for rendering web pages, handling user interactions, and providing an interactive experience. Front-end technologies typically involve HTML, CSS, and JavaScript.

- **Back-End:** The back-end, also known as server-side development, involves the server and database components that manage data, process requests, and interact with the front-end. Common back-end technologies include server-side scripting languages like PHP, Ruby, Python, and databases like MySQL or MongoDB.

10.3.2 Why Integration Matters

Integrating the front-end and back-end is crucial for several reasons:

- **Data Exchange:** To display dynamic content and user-specific information, the front-end must communicate with the back-end to retrieve and update data.

- **User Interactivity:** Users interact with the front-end, triggering actions that often require server-side processing or data storage.

- **Security:** Proper integration helps enforce security measures, such as user authentication and authorization, data validation, and protection against common web vulnerabilities like SQL injection and cross-site scripting (XSS).

- **Scalability:** As your web project grows, the ability to scale both front-end and back-end components is essential to handle increased traffic and data.

10.3.3 Strategies for Integration

Achieving effective front-end and back-end integration requires careful planning and adherence to best practices:

- **APIs (Application Programming Interfaces):** A common approach is to create APIs that allow the front-end to communicate with the back-end. RESTful APIs or GraphQL are popular choices for defining clear, standardized endpoints for data exchange.

- **AJAX (Asynchronous JavaScript and XML):** AJAX allows the front-end to make asynchronous requests to the back-end, enabling dynamic content loading without requiring a full page refresh.

- **Data Formats:** Agree upon data formats such as JSON or XML for transferring data between front-end and back-end components.

- **Authentication and Authorization:** Implement user authentication and authorization mechanisms to control access to protected resources and functionalities.

- **Session Management:** For user sessions and state management, ensure that the front-end and back-end components can maintain session data consistently.

10.3.4 Testing and Debugging Integration

Thoroughly test the integration between the front-end and back-end to identify and resolve issues. Tools like browser developer tools, API testing tools (e.g., Postman), and server logs are valuable for debugging integration problems.

10.3.5 Continuous Integration and Deployment (CI/CD)

Consider implementing CI/CD pipelines to automate the testing and deployment of integrated front-end and back-end code. This helps maintain consistency and reliability in the development process.

Front-end and back-end integration is at the core of building a complete and functional web project. By establishing clear communication channels, defining data exchange formats, and implementing robust security measures, you can create a seamless user experience and ensure that your project functions as intended. Effective integration bridges the gap between the user interface and the server-side operations, resulting in a cohesive and powerful web application or website.

10.4 Testing and Debugging

Testing and debugging are integral parts of web development that ensure your web project functions correctly, is free from errors, and provides an optimal user experience. In this section, we'll delve into the importance of testing and debugging, explore various testing techniques, and discuss debugging strategies to help you create a robust and reliable web project.

10.4.1 The Importance of Testing and Debugging

Testing and debugging serve several critical purposes in web development:

- **Error Detection:** Testing helps identify errors and bugs in your code, whether they are related to functionality, user interface issues, or security vulnerabilities.

- **Quality Assurance:** Rigorous testing ensures that your web project meets the desired standards of quality, functionality, and performance.

- **User Experience:** Thorough testing helps create a positive user experience by preventing issues that might frustrate or confuse users.

- **Security:** Testing can uncover vulnerabilities that may expose your web project to security threats, such as data breaches or malicious attacks.

10.4.2 Testing Techniques

There are various testing techniques you can employ to evaluate different aspects of your web project:

- **Unit Testing:** Test individual components or functions in isolation to ensure they work as expected. JavaScript testing frameworks like Jest or Mocha are commonly used for unit testing.

- **Integration Testing:** Verify that different parts of your web project work together seamlessly. This involves testing interactions between components, modules, or services.

- **Functional Testing:** Assess the overall functionality of your web project by testing user scenarios and use cases. Tools like Selenium or Cypress can automate functional testing.

- **User Interface (UI) Testing:** Ensure that the user interface elements display correctly and function as intended across various browsers and devices. UI testing tools like WebDriver or Puppeteer are helpful for this purpose.

- **Performance Testing:** Evaluate the performance of your web project by measuring factors such as page load times, response times, and resource utilization.

- **Security Testing:** Conduct security assessments to identify and address vulnerabilities, including penetration testing and code reviews for security flaws.

10.4.3 Debugging Strategies

Effective debugging is essential for identifying and resolving issues in your web project. Here are some strategies to streamline the debugging process:

- **Browser Developer Tools:** Most web browsers provide developer tools with debugging capabilities. You can inspect HTML, CSS, and JavaScript, set breakpoints, and view console logs.

- **Logging:** Use console.log() statements strategically to output variable values and messages to the console. This helps trace the flow of your code and identify issues.

- **Code Linters:** Employ code linters like ESLint (JavaScript) or Prettier (HTML/CSS) to catch syntax errors and enforce coding standards.

- **Error Handling:** Implement robust error-handling mechanisms, including try...catch blocks in JavaScript, to gracefully handle exceptions and prevent crashes.

- **Version Control:** Version control systems like Git allow you to track changes in your codebase, making it easier to identify when and where issues were introduced.

- **Peer Review:** Collaborative code reviews with colleagues can uncover problems that may be challenging to spot individually.

10.4.4 Continuous Testing

Incorporating testing into your development workflow is best achieved through continuous testing practices. This involves running tests automatically whenever code changes are committed, ensuring that new code doesn't introduce regressions or break existing functionality.

Testing and debugging are vital aspects of web development that contribute to the success of your web project. By systematically testing your project using various techniques and employing effective debugging strategies, you can create a reliable and user-friendly web application or website that meets both functional and quality standards. Thorough testing and meticulous debugging not only enhance the user experience but also boost the credibility and reliability of your web project.

10.5 Launching Your Website

Congratulations, you've successfully developed and tested your web project, and now it's time to share it with the world. Launching your website is a significant milestone in web development, and it involves several essential steps to ensure your project is accessible, secure, and ready for visitors. In this section, we'll guide you through the process of launching your website.

10.5.1 Web Hosting and Domain Setup

Before you can make your website accessible on the internet, you need to choose a web hosting service and configure your domain name:

- **Web Hosting:** Select a reputable web hosting provider that meets your project's requirements. Shared hosting, virtual private servers (VPS), and cloud hosting are common options. Set up your hosting environment, including server configurations and security settings.

- **Domain Name:** Choose a domain name that reflects your project's identity and purpose. Register the domain through a domain registrar, and configure domain name system (DNS) settings to point to your web hosting server.

10.5.2 Deployment

Deploying your website involves transferring all your web project's files and assets to the web server. You can use various methods for deployment:

- **FTP (File Transfer Protocol):** Use FTP clients like FileZilla to upload files to the server manually.

- **Version Control Deployment:** If you're using version control (e.g., Git), you can set up automated deployment pipelines to push code changes to the server whenever updates are made.

- **Content Management Systems (CMS):** If your website is built on a CMS like WordPress, Joomla, or Drupal, follow the CMS-specific deployment procedures.

10.5.3 Website Security

Security is paramount when launching a website. Take these measures to enhance your website's security:

- **SSL/TLS Certificate:** Install an SSL/TLS certificate to encrypt data exchanged between your website and users' browsers. This provides a secure browsing experience and boosts your website's credibility.

- **Security Plugins and Tools:** Depending on your website's platform, install security plugins or tools to protect against common threats like malware, DDoS attacks, and unauthorized access.

- **Regular Updates:** Keep your web server, CMS, plugins, and themes up to date to patch security vulnerabilities.

- **Backup Strategy:** Implement a robust backup strategy to safeguard your website's data. Regularly back up your files and databases to a secure location.

- **Security Headers:** Configure security headers in your web server to prevent security risks, such as cross-site scripting (XSS) and clickjacking.

10.5.4 Performance Optimization

Optimizing your website's performance ensures fast loading times and a smooth user experience:

- **Caching:** Implement caching mechanisms to store frequently accessed data, reducing server load and improving response times.

- **Content Delivery Network (CDN):** Utilize CDNs to distribute website content across multiple servers worldwide, minimizing latency and speeding up content delivery.

- **Image Optimization:** Compress and optimize images to reduce page load times without compromising quality.

- **Minification:** Minify CSS, JavaScript, and HTML files to reduce their file sizes and improve load times.

10.5.5 Testing in Production

After deploying your website, conduct thorough testing in a production environment to ensure everything works as expected. This includes functionality testing, cross-browser testing, and responsive design validation.

10.5.6 Monitoring and Analytics

Implement website monitoring tools and analytics services to track user behavior, identify issues, and gather insights to improve your website's performance and content.

10.5.7 SEO Optimization

Optimize your website for search engines by following SEO best practices. This includes optimizing meta tags, creating a sitemap, and submitting your site to search engines.

10.5.8 Launch Announcement

Once your website is live, announce its launch through various channels, such as social media, email newsletters, and press releases.

10.5.9 Continuous Maintenance

Website maintenance is an ongoing process. Regularly update content, monitor security, and address issues as they arise.

Engage with user feedback to make improvements and enhancements.

Launching your website marks the culmination of your web development journey. By carefully planning your hosting and domain setup, ensuring security and performance, and conducting thorough testing, you can confidently release your web project to the public. Remember that launching is just the beginning; ongoing maintenance and improvement are essential to keep your website relevant and successful in the long run.

10.6 Post-Launch Maintenance and Updates

Launching your website is a significant accomplishment, but it's only the beginning of your web project's journey. To keep your website running smoothly, secure, and up-to-date, you must establish a post-launch maintenance and update plan. In this section, we'll explore the importance of ongoing maintenance and provide guidelines for keeping your web project in top shape.

10.6.1 Continuous Monitoring

After the launch, monitoring your website's performance, security, and user experience becomes crucial. Here are some key aspects to consider:

- **Performance Monitoring:** Keep an eye on your website's loading times, server response times, and overall performance. Address any performance issues promptly to ensure a seamless user experience.

- **Security Monitoring:** Regularly check for security vulnerabilities, apply security patches, and stay informed about emerging threats. Utilize security plugins and tools to scan for malware and protect against potential breaches.

- **User Feedback:** Encourage user feedback and actively engage with your audience. Listen to user comments, complaints, and suggestions to make necessary improvements.

10.6.2 Content Updates

Your web project's content should remain fresh and relevant to your audience. Consider the following:

- **Regular Content Review:** Periodically review and update the content on your website. Ensure that information, products, or services are accurate and up-to-date.

- **Blogging and Publishing:** If you have a blog or news section, maintain a consistent publishing schedule to provide valuable, current content to your visitors.

- **SEO Optimization:** Continuously optimize your content for search engines by using relevant keywords, meta tags, and other SEO techniques.

10.6.3 Software and Plugin Updates

Web technologies evolve, and so do the tools and software used in your web project:

- **CMS Updates:** If your website is built on a content management system (CMS) like WordPress or Joomla, regularly update both the core CMS and plugins or extensions. These updates often include security patches and feature enhancements.

- **Server Software:** Keep server software, including web server software (e.g., Apache, Nginx), up to date to benefit from performance improvements and security fixes.

- **Third-Party Integrations:** If your website integrates with third-party services or APIs, ensure that these integrations remain compatible with updates and changes from those providers.

10.6.4 Backups and Disaster Recovery

Maintain a robust backup and disaster recovery strategy:

- **Regular Backups:** Continue to back up your website's files and databases regularly. Store backups securely in multiple locations.

- **Disaster Recovery Plan:** Develop a disaster recovery plan to handle unexpected events such as server crashes, data loss, or security breaches.

10.6.5 User Experience Enhancements

Improve the user experience to keep visitors engaged and satisfied:

- **Usability Testing:** Conduct usability tests to identify areas where users may encounter difficulties or frustration. Make necessary adjustments to enhance usability.

- **Performance Optimization:** Continue to optimize your website's performance, especially as it grows and accumulates more content.

- **Responsive Design:** Ensure that your website remains responsive and functional across various devices and screen sizes.

10.6.6 Security Measures

Security should be an ongoing concern:

- **Regular Audits:** Conduct periodic security audits to identify vulnerabilities and assess your website's overall security posture.

- **User Authentication:** If your website requires user accounts, regularly review and update authentication methods to enhance security.

- **Monitoring and Incident Response:** Implement continuous monitoring and incident response protocols to detect and respond to security threats promptly.

10.6.7 User Engagement and Marketing

Engage with your audience and promote your web project:

- **Social Media:** Maintain an active presence on social media platforms to interact with users, share updates, and promote new content or products.

- **Email Marketing:** Use email newsletters and campaigns to stay in touch with subscribers and drive traffic to your website.

10.6.8 Compliance and Regulations

Stay informed about legal and regulatory changes that may affect your website:

- **Privacy Regulations:** Comply with data protection regulations such as GDPR or CCPA if they apply to your website. Review and update privacy policies and consent mechanisms as needed.

10.6.9 Documentation

Keep thorough documentation of your web project's architecture, configurations, and changes. This documentation will be invaluable for troubleshooting and future development.

Post-launch maintenance and updates are essential to keep your web project thriving. By continuously monitoring, updating, and enhancing your website, you can provide an optimal user experience, ensure security, and stay competitive in the ever-evolving online landscape. A well-maintained website not only retains existing users but also attracts new ones, contributing to the long-term success of your web project.

11 Conclusion

"Web Development with HTML, CSS, and JavaScript" has been your comprehensive guide to the world of web development. Throughout this book, we've explored the fundamental concepts, techniques, and best practices that are essential for anyone looking to become a proficient web developer. Whether you're a beginner taking your first steps into the web development landscape or an experienced coder looking to refresh your skills, this book has provided you with valuable insights and knowledge.

In this journey, we've covered a wide range of topics, from the basics of HTML, CSS, and JavaScript to more advanced concepts like responsive design, web accessibility, and front-end frameworks. We've discussed the importance of testing, debugging, and maintaining your web projects to ensure they remain secure, efficient, and user-friendly.

Web development is a dynamic field that constantly evolves with new technologies and trends. As you embark on your own web development projects or pursue a career in this exciting industry, remember that learning is an ongoing process. Stay curious, keep experimenting, and continue to explore the ever-changing landscape of web technologies.

By following the principles and techniques outlined in this book and staying up-to-date with the latest developments in web development, you are well-equipped to create exceptional websites and web applications that engage users, meet their needs, and make a positive impact on the digital world.

Whether you're building personal projects, contributing to open-source initiatives, or working on professional websites for clients or employers, your journey as a web developer is a rewarding one. The skills you've acquired from this book provide a solid foundation upon which you can build and expand your expertise, making your mark in the dynamic and ever-expanding realm of web development.

Thank you for joining us on this educational journey, and we wish you success and fulfillment in all your web development endeavors. Keep coding, keep learning, and keep pushing the boundaries of what the web can achieve!

11.1 Future Trends in Web Development

As we conclude our journey through the world of web development with HTML, CSS, and JavaScript, it's important to look ahead and consider the exciting future trends that will shape the industry. Web development is a field that constantly evolves, driven by technological advancements and changing user expectations. Here are some of the key trends that are likely to influence the future of web development:

- **Progressive Web Apps (PWAs):** PWAs combine the best of web and mobile apps, offering fast loading times, offline capabilities, and a native app-like experience. Expect to see more websites adopting PWA principles to enhance user engagement.

- **Single Page Applications (SPAs):** SPAs, powered by JavaScript frameworks like React, Angular, and Vue.js, provide seamless and responsive user experiences by loading content dynamically. SPAs are likely to become even more prevalent, particularly for web applications.

- **WebAssembly (Wasm):** WebAssembly is a binary instruction format that allows languages like C, C++, and Rust to run in web browsers at near-native speed.

This technology opens the door to high-performance web applications and games.

- **Web Components:** Web Components are a set of web platform APIs that allow you to create reusable and encapsulated custom HTML elements. This trend promotes modularity, reusability, and maintainability in web development.

- **Voice User Interfaces (VUIs):** With the rise of smart speakers and virtual assistants, voice interactions are becoming a significant aspect of web development. Building voice-activated features and optimizing websites for voice search will be essential.

- **Artificial Intelligence (AI) and Machine Learning (ML):** AI and ML are increasingly being integrated into web applications for tasks like personalization, recommendation systems, and chatbots. Expect AI-driven web experiences to become more sophisticated.

- **Web 3.0 and Decentralized Technologies:** Blockchain and decentralized applications (DApps) are challenging the centralized nature of the web. These technologies are likely to reshape how data is stored, transactions are conducted, and identity is managed online.

- **Augmented Reality (AR) and Virtual Reality (VR):** AR and VR technologies are expanding beyond gaming and entertainment to create immersive web experiences.

They have the potential to revolutionize e-commerce, education, and training.

- **Enhanced Web Security:** With an increasing focus on cybersecurity, web developers will continue to implement stronger security measures, including more robust encryption, authentication methods, and threat detection systems.

- **Web Accessibility:** Accessibility is not just a trend but a fundamental aspect of web development. As awareness grows, web developers will increasingly prioritize creating accessible web experiences for all users.

- **Cross-Platform Development:** Developing web applications that work seamlessly across various platforms, including desktop, mobile, and even IoT devices, will remain a priority as the digital ecosystem continues to expand.

- **Sustainability and Performance:** As concerns about the environmental impact of the web grow, web developers will emphasize optimizing website performance and reducing carbon footprints through efficient coding and server usage.

The future of web development is bright and filled with opportunities for innovation. Embracing these trends and staying adaptable will be essential for web developers to create cutting-edge web experiences that cater to the evolving needs of users and businesses. As you continue your journey in web development, keep an open mind, stay curious, and be ready to embrace new technologies and techniques that come your way. The world of web development will continue to be an exciting and dynamic space, and your skills and creativity will play a vital role in shaping its future.

11.2 Resources for Further Learning

Congratulations on completing this book on web development with HTML, CSS, and JavaScript! You've gained a solid foundation in web development, but the journey is far from over. The world of web development is ever-evolving, and there's always more to learn and explore. Here are some valuable resources to continue your learning and stay up-to-date with the latest developments in web development:

11.2.1 Online Courses and Tutorials

- **Coursera:** Offers a wide range of web development courses from top universities and institutions.
- **edX:** Provides courses on web development, including front-end and back-end development.
- **Codecademy:** Offers interactive coding lessons for HTML, CSS, JavaScript, and more.
- **freeCodeCamp:** Offers a free, self-paced curriculum covering web development, including hands-on coding challenges.

11.2.2 Books

- **"Eloquent JavaScript" by Marijn Haverbeke:** A comprehensive book that delves deep into JavaScript.
- **"CSS: The Definitive Guide" by Eric A. Meyer and Estelle Weyl:** An extensive resource for CSS.
- **"HTML and CSS: Design and Build Websites" by Jon Duckett:** A beginner-friendly guide to HTML and CSS.
- **"You Don't Know JS" by Kyle Simpson:** A series of books that cover JavaScript in-depth.

11.2.3 Documentation

- **Mozilla Developer Network (MDN):** An extensive resource for web developers, including detailed documentation for HTML, CSS, and JavaScript.
- **W3Schools:** Provides tutorials and references for web technologies, including HTML, CSS, and JavaScript.

11.2.4 Forums and Communities

- **Stack Overflow:** A vibrant community where you can ask questions, seek solutions, and learn from experienced developers.
- **GitHub:** Explore open-source projects, collaborate with others, and contribute to web development projects.

11.2.5 Web Development Blogs and Newsletters

- **Smashing Magazine:** Offers articles, tutorials, and insights on web design and development.
- **CSS-Tricks:** A valuable resource for CSS-related tips and tricks.
- **A List Apart:** Focuses on web design, development, and content strategy.

11.2.6 YouTube Channels

- **The Net Ninja:** Provides video tutorials on web development topics, including JavaScript frameworks.
- **Traversy Media:** Offers a wide range of web development tutorials and courses.

11.2.7 Coding Challenges and Practice

- **LeetCode:** Offers coding challenges and competitions to enhance your coding skills.
- **HackerRank:** Provides coding challenges and competitions for web developers.

11.2.8 Podcasts

- **ShopTalk Show:** Discusses web design, development, and UX.
- **JavaScript Jabber:** Focuses on JavaScript and related technologies.

11.2.9 Conferences and Meetups

- Attend web development conferences and meetups in your area or participate in virtual events.

11.2.10 Online Platforms

- Explore online coding platforms like CodePen and JSFiddle to experiment with HTML, CSS, and JavaScript in real-time.

Remember that the web development community is vast and supportive. Don't hesitate to reach out for help, collaborate on projects, and share your knowledge with others. Continuous learning and practice are key to becoming a proficient web developer, and the resources mentioned here will help you on your journey to mastering web development. Keep coding, stay curious, and embrace the exciting challenges and opportunities that lie ahead in the world of web development!